"I've been reading Kevin DeYoung since we were both young and restless. Over countless articles and books, he's helped me mature in my view of the world and understanding of God's word. *Impossible Christianity* challenged some of my assumptions and corrected some of my misconceptions. I know it can help you enjoy the pleasure of God in a quiet and dignified life."

Collin Hansen, Executive Director, The Keller Center for Cultural Apologetics

"Read it to the end—where we find a benediction. But from the beginning, this book aims to bless God's people by sending us out to live in daily obedience to the Lord who has saved us. Kevin DeYoung is not simplistic, but he makes the call of Christ on our lives much simpler (and much more biblical) than the cacophony of voices around us might suggest."

Kathleen Nielson, author, speaker

"*Impossible Christianity* addresses most of the difficult questions about what the Christian life looks like. It tackles objections and difficulties head-on. DeYoung challenges issues most of us would be reluctant to confront. You may not agree with all his conclusions, but you will be forced to come up with biblical arguments to refute them, and that will prove difficult. This is one of those books that will be talked about for some time. Exceptionally clear, forthright, and engaging."

Derek W. H. Thomas, Senior Minister, First Presbyterian Church, Columbia, South Carolina; Chancellor's Professor, Reformed Theological Seminary; Teaching Fellow, Ligonier Ministries

"This book is for the Christian who believes low-level guilt and a slightly disturbed conscience are normal (even right!), and who may rely on that bad feeling as a bit of proof that they are, in fact, virtuous. DeYoung is here to remind you that Jesus set you free so that you really can please your good heavenly Father with a clean conscience. God smiles at the ordinary efforts of his children."

Abigail Dodds, author, *Bread of Life*; *(A)Typical Woman*; and *A Student's Guide to Womanhood*

Impossible Christianity

Other Crossway Books by Kevin DeYoung

The Biggest Story: How the Snake Crusher Brings Us Back to the Garden (2015)

The Biggest Story ABC (2017)

Crazy Busy: A (Mercifully) Short Book about a (Really) Big Problem (2013)

Don't Call It a Comeback: The Old Faith for a New Day (2011)

Grace Defined and Defended: What a 400-Year-Old Confession Teaches Us about Sin, Salvation, and the Sovereignty of God (2019)

The Hole in Our Holiness: Filling the Gap between Gospel Passion and the Pursuit of Godliness (2012)

The Lord's Prayer: Learning from Jesus on What, Why, and How to Pray (2022)

Men and Women in the Church: A Short, Biblical, Practical Introduction (2021)

Taking God at His Word: Why the Bible Is Knowable, Necessary, and Enough, and What That Means for You and Me (2014)

The Ten Commandments: What They Mean, Why They Matter, and Why We Should Obey Them (2018)

What Does the Bible Really Teach about Homosexuality? (2015)

What Is the Mission of the Church?: Making Sense of Social Justice, Shalom, and the Great Commission (coauthor; 2011)

Impossible
Christianity

Why Following Jesus Does Not Mean You Have to Change
the World, Be an Expert in Everything, Accept Spiritual
Failure, and Feel Miserable Pretty Much All the Time

Kevin DeYoung

WHEATON, ILLINOIS

Impossible Christianity: Why Following Jesus Does Not Mean You Have to Change the World, Be an Expert in Everything, Accept Spiritual Failure, and Feel Miserable Pretty Much All the Time

Copyright © 2023 by Kevin DeYoung

Published by Crossway
        1300 Crescent Street
        Wheaton, Illinois 60187

Published in association with the literary agency of Wolgemuth & Associates

Cover design: Jordan Singer

First printing 2023

Printed in the United States of America

Hardcover ISBN: 978-1-4335-8534-0
ePub ISBN: 978-1-4335-8529-6
PDF ISBN: 978-1-4335-8535-7

Library of Congress Cataloging-in-Publication Data

Names: DeYoung, Kevin, author.
Title: Impossible Christianity : why following Jesus does not mean you have to change the world, be an expert in everything, accept spiritual failure, and feel miserable pretty much all the time / Kevin DeYoung.
Description: Wheaton, Illinois : Crossway, 2023. | Includes bibliographical references and index.
Identifiers: LCCN 2022046441 (print) | LCCN 2022046442 (ebook) | ISBN 9781433585340 (hardcover) | ISBN 9781433585357 (pdf) | ISBN 9781433585296 (epub)
Subjects: LCSH: Self-actualization—Religious aspects—Christianity. | Christian life. | God (Christianity)—Worship and love.
Classification: LCC BV4598.2 .D49 2023 (print) | LCC BV4598.2 (ebook) | DDC 248.4—dc23/eng/20230419
LC record available at https://lccn.loc.gov/2022046441
LC ebook record available at https://lccn.loc.gov/2022046442

Crossway is a publishing ministry of Good News Publishers.

LB   32   31   30   29   28   27   26   25   24   23
15   14   13   12   11   10   9   8   7   6   5   4   3   2   1

To my parents

Thank you for loving Christ, loving the church,
loving your kids, and loving each other

Contents

Introduction

Is Christianity Supposed to Feel Impossible?

I'VE ALWAYS LIKED RUNNING, though running hasn't always liked me back.

It might be hard to tell from my intimidating physical presence today, but I wasn't a great athlete as a kid. I played a lot of right field in baseball and spent most innings putting grass in my hat. I played goalie in soccer and stood so far in the back of the net that every ball I stopped was already a goal. I played one year of football and never once touched anyone (which might have been great, except I was on defense). I fractured both of my wrists playing intramural basketball. I got multiple concussions playing hockey. I think I even struck out in kickball.

But I wasn't terrible at running. Back when I was a kid—when parents and educators were less concerned about young people experiencing crushing failure in life—we had to take the annual Presidential Physical Fitness test. The test, at least the one our school conducted, was a combination of push-ups, sit-ups, pull-ups, a standing broad jump, a rope climb, a flexibility test, and a mile run. Compared to the other boys in my grade, I was average to below average in most events. Rope climb was my particular nemesis. ("Hey kid, climb this rope to the top of your three-story gym. Don't worry, there is a small, thin mat on the ground in case you fall from 25 feet. And if you make it to the top, you can ring a bell and then burn the inside of your thighs as you slide back down to earth.") Considering how middling I was overall, and how much I desperately wanted President Reagan to recognize my physical fitness, I was pleasantly surprised when I was one of the first boys to finish the mile run.

I decided that afternoon that running was going to be my thing. Most young men dream of being in the NBA or the NFL. My dream was to come from behind in the anchor leg of the 4 x 400 relay and win the gold medal for Team USA. I always wanted to line up at the start of a race and know that I could run faster than everyone else around me. I never did line up with that feeling because it never was close to the reality. If Eric Liddell felt God's pleasure when he ran, I often felt God saying to me, "Don't quit your day job." But still,

I will always remember running around the baseball diamond and soccer fields at my elementary school and feeling proud that I beat most of the jocks in my grade.

That was over thirty-five years ago, and since then I've worked hard at running, with only the mildest of success. I ran through the cold Michigan winter as a junior high school student in order to get ready for my first season of real running. I notched a 2:35 in the 800 meter as an eighth grader. I looked at our high school record—an impressive 1:55 at the big public school I attended—and set my four-year goal. All I had to do was drop 10 seconds a year, and I'd have the school record as a senior. I met that goal my freshman year and my sophomore year. And that was about it. Turns out the last 20 seconds are a lot harder to trim than the first 20 seconds.

With discipline and hard work and a naturally skinny (I prefer "athletic") frame, I have managed, at times, to be the best of the second-tier runners, or, on occasion, the worst of the pretty good runners. I was all-county JV in cross-country as a sophomore in high school, before injuries derailed my final two years. In track, I was so "good" that I think I tried every event at least once. I eventually settled in to the 110-meter high hurdles, where long legs and decent form could make up for a natural lack of speed. I won a couple races and competed one year in college. Sure, the school was NCAA

Division III, but I am an NCAA letter winner, a fact I have mentioned to my uninterested family many times. I made the conference finals in the hurdles and finished last. Like I said, the worst of the pretty good.

Now firmly ensconced in middle age, I continue to run and exercise regularly. I've read dozens of books about running. I've watched scores of YouTube videos and more track-and-field meets on TV than literally anyone I know. I've purchased lots of good running gear—from shoes to hats to singlets to special socks to short shorts (too short, my wife says). I've done road races and triathlons of various distances. Sometimes I finish near the top of my age group. Sometimes I barely finish. If you compare me to someone getting off the couch to run a Thanksgiving turkey trot, I'm pretty good. If you compare me to serious runners, I am, well, not a serious runner. I'm doing the best I can with my limited time, my limited ability, and my limited opportunities. The good news is, if my 5K time doesn't get any slower over the next thirty years, I'll be world class.

Christianity Possible

At this point, some of you are thinking, "More running stories, please!" while the other 99 percent are wishing I would have sprained my ankle and never finished that elementary school mile (don't worry, I've sprained my ankle plenty of times). But believe it or not, my experience with running has everything to do with the title of this book. Many Christians have come to expect (and accept) that being a disciple of Jesus is a lot like my thirty-five-year journey with running. You read the books. You watch the videos. You get the right equipment. You try to be disciplined. You try to improve. But with only the mildest of success.

Maybe you have been following Jesus for many years, maybe since you were a little kid. Sometimes you feel like a winner, but mostly you feel like you are an average to below-average believer. You aren't ready to quit being a Christian. You know that being a Christian is important. In fact, it's the most important thing in your life. You like being a Christian and are willing to work hard at it. The only trouble is, Christianity seems impossible.

I should hasten to add an important clarification, lest you misunderstand what this book is about. You may think, "Ah, so this is another book about how justification is by faith alone, another book about how the gospel is good news for exhausted people, another book about how God loves us even though we are spiritual failures." Not exactly. I *do* believe in justification by faith alone—with all my heart, soul, mind, and strength. I *do* believe that the gospel is good news for exhausted people—and many of us are dog-tired. But that's not what this book is about, at least not directly. This book is about the last line of that sentence above, the line about "how God loves us even though we are spiritual failures." This book is about how that line, however well intentioned, is unbiblical, inaccurate, and unhelpful.

You and I are sometimes confused about what it means to follow Jesus. To be sure, we do not earn merit with God. As fallen creatures, we will never be good enough to make it to heaven. Salvation is all of grace from start to finish. But reveling in God's grace does not mean we should revel in being spiritual failures. He does not mean for us to feel bad all the time. He does not mean for us to be lackluster disciples. He does not mean for us to be constantly overwhelmed. He does not mean for us to feel guilty all the time. God does not mean for Christianity to be impossible.

Many Christians have resigned themselves to the fact—or at least it seems like a fact—that they will be failures as followers of Jesus. Forgiven, yes. Justified, yes. On their way to heaven, yes. But as disciples and Christians, nothing special. Just like my running career, we will work hard and enjoy a few modest accomplishments. We will do the best we can with our limited time, our limited ability, and our limited opportunities. And yet we will never have the requisite gifts to be truly successful. We will not perfectly keep the Ten Commandments. We will not fully live out the Sermon on the Mount. We will never pray enough. We will never give enough. We will never share our faith enough. We will not renew our city. We will not repair all that ails our nation. We will not change the world.

I once heard a well-known Christian writer claim that every author really has only one book. I hope that's not exactly true, but he was certainly correct to suggest that most authors have one big idea that finds its way into almost everything they write. As I think about the other books I've written, it occurs to me that the explicit theme of this book has been an implicit theme in many of my other books; namely, that following Christ is never easy, but it does not have to be impenetrably mysterious, exceedingly complex, and relentlessly guilt-producing. Normal people can walk in God's will (*Just Do Something*) and live a holy life (*The Hole in Our Holiness*) without being frantic all the time (*Crazy Busy*). Normal churches are worth celebrating (*Why We Love the Church*), and the mission of the church is not everything under the sun (*What Is the Mission of the Church?*). Ordinary Christians and ordinary churches can be faithful, fruitful, and pleasing to God. In short, Christianity doesn't have to be impossible.

The Race We All Must Run

Recently, my ten-year-old daughter ran a local 5K race with her good friend of the same age. They were extremely excited and nervous for their first race. Before my daughter left for the race, I looked her in the eye and said to her, with feigned intensity so she knew I was kind of serious and kind of joking, "I want you to remember three things. Jesus loves you. I love you. And you're a DeYoung." It was my over-the-top dad way of letting her know that I was proud of her and that she was going to do a great job. Of course, she didn't qualify for the Olympics, and she wasn't the fastest one out there. She stopped to walk once or twice. But she *did* do a great job. She wasn't a failure. I wasn't lying when I said I loved her and praised her for running so far and so fast. What dad would tell his little girl anything else?

True, if she keeps running, she'll try to get better. Maybe she'll be better than her brothers. Maybe she will be at the back of the pack. Either way, if she runs in the right way and for the right reasons, I'll be proud. She won't be a failure in my eyes. And we don't have to live like we are failures in God's eyes either. He saves us by his grace, gives us a new name, and then tells us to set aside every weight and run the race set before us, with a great cloud of witnesses cheering us along the way (Heb. 12:1).

Following Christ entails suffering and endurance. The call of Christian discipleship is a costly (and liberating) summons to die to ourselves. Christianity is neither simple nor pain free. But following Jesus does not mean signing up for the Impossible Missions Force. Humility does not mean we should feel miserable all the time; meekness is not the same as spiritual failurism. The Spirit works within us. The word moves among us. The love of Christ compels us. "Who is it that overcomes the world except the one who believes that Jesus is the Son of God?" (1 John 5:5).

As Christians, we have a race to be run, *and* it can be run. This is a recurring theme in Paul's letters (so if you don't like running analogies, blame him). Paul ran purposefully, with discipline and self-control. He knew the race could be run poorly, but he also knew how to keep from being disqualified (1 Cor. 9:26–27). As he came to the end of his life—an imperfect life filled with sin and struggle—Paul did not hesitate to conclude that he had fought the good fight, he had finished the race, and he had kept the faith (2 Tim. 4:7). This "chief of sinners" understood that there was laid up for him the crown of righteousness, which the Lord, the righteous judge, would award to him on that day, and not only to him but also to all who loved the Lord's appearing (4:8). Paul did not consider the Christian race a hopeless labyrinth or an ultramarathon that only the few and the fittest could survive. He believed the race he was on—the race he completed—to be a privilege. He also believed it was possible.

1

How (Not) to Make Christianity Possible

YES, *CHARIOTS OF FIRE* is my favorite movie. With running and missions and Scottish accents, how could it not be? But if *Chariots of Fire* is my all-time favorite, the movie *Babe* is definitely in my top ten.

Babe is a farm pig who wants to be a sheepdog. Although the other animals look down on Babe, and the people in the sheepdog world find him an embarrassment, Babe's boss, Farmer Hoggett, believes in him. At the movie's climax, Farmer Hoggett signs Babe up for a national sheepdog competition. Everything is stacked against Babe. The farmer's wife is mortified, the crowds laugh in derision, and the sheepdog judges only begrudgingly accept Babe into the competition based on a technicality. The poor pig struggles until Rex the dog races home and back again to give Babe the secret password for talking to the sheep (okay, so it may not be based on real-life events).

The ending of the movie is just perfect. With great patience and kindness, Babe speaks to the sheep, and the sheep obey his voice. The gruff sheep execute the instructions flawlessly. And as they return to the sheep pen, and the gate clicks behind them, the crowd erupts in acclamation and applause. The final shot shows Babe sitting next to Farmer Hoggett—the pig looking up at him, and the farmer looking down at his special sheepdog. Then Hoggett, with a satisfied grin, closes the movie with these words: "That'll do, Pig. That'll do."[1]

Well Done, Good and Faithful Servant

This book is about whether it is possible to live our lives as Christians such that God the Father looks down on us, smiles, and says, "That'll do, my child. That'll do."

We know that God accepts us in Christ, that we can be justified by faith, that we can be forgiven because of the sacrifice of Christ on the cross. But this book is not about getting to heaven. This book is about whether on our way to heaven

---

1 *Babe*, directed by Chris Noonan (Universal City, CA: Universal Pictures, 1995).

we are doomed to a life of guilt, impossible standards, and failure. Is it possible for the Christian not only to be forgiven of his sins but to live a faithful and forgiven life so that when he reaches heaven's shore, God will greet him there with the words "Well done!"?

We know this is possible because the Bible tells us so. In the parable of the talents, Jesus tells the story of a man who goes on a journey and entrusts his servants with his property (Matt. 25:14–30). The master gave to one servant five talents, to another, two talents, and to the third, one talent (and remember, a talent is not an ability, like we use the word, but a monetary unit). After a long time, the master returned and settled accounts with his servants. The first servant made five talents in addition to the five he had been given. Likewise, the second servant made two more talents. But the third servant, fearing that his master was overdemanding and hard-charging, buried his talent in the ground so that at least he wouldn't lose what he had been given. To the first two servants, the master proclaims, "Well done, good and faithful servant" (25:21, 23), but the third man is called a "wicked and slothful servant" (25:26).

Notice three things about this parable.

First, this is not a story (just) for pastors and missionaries or world-famous Christians. This is about life in the kingdom

(Matt. 25:1) and how God will assess us at the end of the age (25:13). "Well done" is what ordinary Christians will hear, not a select few superradical believers.

Second, the two good servants were commended for being faithful with what they had been given. The first servant produced five talents, and the second servant produced two talents, but they were both given the same commendation. They weren't expected to do what they couldn't do. The master didn't demand any more, or expect any less, than faithfulness with the opportunities they had.

Third, the last servant went off track because he thought he served an impossible master. We might think that the servant would work extra hard because he considered his master difficult and unfair. But the servant's fear made him lazy. He didn't work hard. He didn't think creatively. He didn't do the best he could with what he had been given. Instead, he played it safe. He knew he was likely to fail, so he didn't even try.

Surely these are important lessons for us. Being a disciple of Jesus is not easy, but when we think Christianity is impossible, we normally don't do more for Christ; we do less. We give up without much of a fight, figuring that even if God acquits us as Judge, he can never be pleased with us as Father. True, the master in the parable owned his hard reputation, but this was to shame the servant for not investing his money with the bankers—the least he should have done if his view of the master was accurate. The first two servants didn't encounter a hard and unreasonable master, and there is no indication they expected him to be so. They experienced the master as generous, encouraging, and rewarding. They didn't live in dreaded fear of the master. They were faithful servants who, like us, knew that it was possible for the master to smile down on them and say, "That'll do, friends. That'll do."

Guardrails for the Journey

No one devised a plan to conceive of Christian discipleship in such a way that most disciples would feel like perpetual *D-* followers of Jesus who get most things wrong and never do the right things as well as they should. And yet many Christians have accepted their fate as that's just what Christianity is like. We have commandments to obey, but we will never obey them. We have more spiritual tasks than we have time. We struggle to read our Bible every day, and we are even worse at prayer. We don't evangelize enough, and we don't give enough money away. We carry around the guilt of our fathers, and we can't do anything to get rid of it. God justifies sinners like us—that's good. But all we'll ever do in this life is sin. God may forgive us, but he doesn't like us. Beatific vision later, blessed failurism now.

How did we get here?

One of the reasons we think this way about Christianity is that there are other truths we want to make sure we *don't* think. That is to say, Christianity became impossible, in large part, because of our good intentions to emphasize a host of truths that, taken together, make it *seem* like devout piety requires an impossible Christianity. And it's true: there are wrong ways to make Christianity "possible." If we are not careful, we will end up conceiving of Christian faith and Christian obedience and Christian salvation in ways that are sub-Christian. So before I go any further in arguing against impossible Christianity, I need to put some guardrails in place—not walls that prevent us from seeing the truth, but guardrails that keep us on the narrow path that leads to truth.

With that in mind, here are seven things I am *not* saying in this book.

Mistake #1: We Can Be Good Enough to Get into Heaven

The Bible is crystal clear on this point: apart from Christ, there is no one righteous, no not one (Rom. 3:10). All have sinned and fall short of the glory of God (3:23). Consequently, "we hold that one is justified by faith apart from works of the law" (3:28). As George Whitefield put it, we could sooner climb to the moon by a rope of sand as we could be justified by our works. We are all born into this world with inherited guilt and inherited depravity (Rom. 5:12–21). We must be born again by God's sovereign and unilateral initiative (John 1:12–13; 3:5; 6:44). In saying Christianity is possible I am not saying—and may I be accursed if I were ever to say—that we can merit eternal life or that we can add anything to the finished work of Christ on our behalf (Gal. 1:8). We are saved by grace through faith. This is not our own doing; it is the gift of God, not a result of works, so that no one may boast (Eph. 2:8–9).

Mistake #2: Christians Can Be Perfect

When I was in college, my fellow students and I were sometimes accosted on our way to class by a street preacher telling us to repent and believe in Christ. I wanted to appreciate the man. He wasn't a jerk, and much of what he said was true. He took sin seriously and called students to turn from sin and put their faith in Jesus. But he also preached a message of perfectionism. He was adamant that true Christians could be, and should be, free from conscious sin. This is positively *not* what this book is about. If personal experience weren't enough to convince of indwelling sin, the Bible tells us that "there is not a righteous man on earth who does good and never sins" (Eccl. 7:20). Quite the contrary. "If we say we have no sin, we deceive ourselves, and the truth is not in us" (1 John 1:8). While we can do that which is *truly* good, we will never (on earth) be fully and perfectly good. In fact, the closer we get to Jesus, the more obvious our sins will become.

Mistake #3: Sin Is Not a Big Deal

Once the first two mistakes are ruled out, some Christians assume (or implicitly teach) that sin is nothing to worry about. Obviously, God doesn't like sin, and, all else being equal, he'd rather we didn't sin. But when we do sin, he tussles our hair and gives us a wry grin as if to say, "Silly boy, be more careful next time." This impulse has long been a danger in the church. It's often called "antinomianism," which means "against law." Historically, almost no antinomians have actually taught that God's commands can be ignored and that sin is okay. Antinomianism is more of an attitude that minimizes the need for (and possibility of) obedience and the seriousness of sin even for justified believers. But God is not blind to our disobedience. He does not offer us three free sins. The letters of Paul and Peter and John, not to mention Jesus's letters to the seven churches in Revelation, are filled with exhortations—to Christians and to churches—to repent and warnings for those who do not.

Mistake #4: Being a Christian Is Trouble-Free

If we think following Jesus involves no fight and no struggle, we haven't read our Bible carefully (or at all!). Being a Christian means entering by the narrow gate (Matt. 7:13); it means striving to enter the narrow door (Luke 13:24); it means putting to death the deeds of the body (Rom. 8:13); it means wrestling against cosmic powers and demonic principalities (Eph. 6:12); it means fighting the good fight of faith (1 Tim. 6:12); it means making every effort to supplement our faith with virtue and godliness and all the qualities of holiness (2 Pet. 1:5–7). Possible Christianity is not passive Christianity.

Mistake #5: We Should Stop So Being Hard on Ourselves

This can be good advice. Some Christians experience misplaced shame. Some Christians have consciences that are too tender. Some Christians have never given themselves permission to succeed with God-pleasing obedience. But as automatic counsel for everyone in every situation, this advice is unhelpful, if not downright heretical. There are plenty of books and blogs out there basically telling us, "You're awesome. You're beautiful. You may be a screwup, but so what? We all are. And if people don't love you just the way you are, that's their problem. Don't let anyone tell you that your desires are wrong, or your family is dysfunctional, or your divorce is unbiblical, or your eating habits are unhealthy, or your beliefs are unorthodox, or your behavior is unChristian." That message sells—big time. But it's not the message that tells us to put off the old self with its practices (Col. 3:9) or to pursue the holiness without which no one will see the Lord (Heb. 12:14). It's not the message Jesus preached when he said, "The time is fulfilled, and the kingdom of God is at hand; repent and believe in the gospel" (Mark 1:15).

Mistake #6: There Is No Cost to Following Jesus

The fact that we serve a crucified Savior should put an end to this misconception straightaway. Since the world hated Jesus, we should expect that it will hate us too (John 15:18–19). We should not be surprised at the fiery trial that comes to test (1 Pet. 4:12). After all, everyone who desires to live a godly life in Christ Jesus will be persecuted (2 Tim. 3:12). To say that Christianity is possible is not to suggest that we float to heaven on flowery beds of ease. Like the man who desires to build a tower has to first check his materials, or like a king on his way to battle must first check the readiness of his troops, we must count the cost before signing up as for Team Jesus (Luke 14:25–33). "If anyone would come after me," Jesus told his disciples, "let him deny himself and take up his cross and follow me" (Matt. 16:24).

Mistake #7: God Will Never Call You to Take Any Risks

One hundred percent safety is not a realistic goal in a fallen world. Every day people get into bad accidents (even with seat belts), they get sick (even with masks), they get burned in a job or a relationship (even though they did due diligence ahead of time). We are finite people who lack knowledge in all sorts of areas. Most notably, we do not know the future. As a result, life is full of risks, even for God's people. Maybe *especially* for God's people. Esther did her part "for such a time as this," even though she knew she might perish in the process (Est. 4:14–16). Shadrach, Meshach, and Abednego refused to bow before Nebuchadnezzar's idol, not knowing if God would deliver them from the fiery furnace (Dan. 3:17–18). Being a faithful follower of Jesus is possible but rarely predictable.

The Road That Lies Between

It may seem, after all that, that we are back at square one, consigned to live a life of sinful failure where we never do enough and we never measure up. But that is not the road these guardrails are meant to protect.

- True, salvation is all of grace. But the grace that saves in justification will also transform us in sanctification (2 Cor. 3:18).

- True, we will never be perfect and sinless here on earth. But we can do that which is genuinely good and pleasing to God (Rom. 12:1–2).

- True, sin is always offensive to a holy God. But we can also repent of sin and know the blessing of a clean conscience and the smile of God (Num. 6:24–26).

- True, being a Christian is hard. But that doesn't mean Christ's yoke can't be easy (Matt. 11:30).

- True, we have to deal honestly with our continuing sin and disobedience. But that doesn't mean we can never do anything that is righteous and obedient (Luke 1:6).

- True, following Jesus means carrying a cross. But it also means finding our life by losing it (Matt. 16:25).

- True, God is going to ask us to do some difficult things. But God is also in the business of doing more than we can ask or imagine (Eph. 3:20).

The Christian life is harder and easier than we think—harder because dying to ourselves, wrestling with the devil, and being hated by the world do not come to us naturally. But it is also easier, because God doesn't insist that we need multiple degrees, thirty hours a day, and superhuman organizational skills to be Jesus's disciples. In the simplest terms, all Jesus asks is that we trust him enough to walk with him, listen to him, and depend on him for everything. No doubt, that is a narrow path and hard way, which is why few are on it. But true disciples *do* walk that road because they know that it is good, and they know that it leads to life.

2

Who Is It That Overcomes the World?

WHENEVER I COUNSEL Christians who are looking for assurance of salvation, I take them to 1 John. This brief epistle is full of help for determining whether we are in the faith. In particular, there are three road signs John gives so we can discern whether we are on the right track. You can think of these three marks as helping us answer the question, Do I have confidence or condemnation?

The first sign is theological. You should have confidence if you believe in Jesus Christ the Son of God (1 John 5:11–13). John doesn't want people to be doubting. God wants you to have assurance, to know that you have eternal life. And this is the first sign, that you believe in Jesus. You believe he is the Christ (2:22). You believe he is the Son of God (5:10). And you believe that Jesus Christ has come in the flesh (4:2). If you get your theology about Jesus all wrong, you will not have eternal life. But one of the signs that should give you confidence before God is that you believe in his only Son Jesus Christ our Lord (4:14–16; 5:1, 5).

The second sign is moral. You should have confidence if you live a righteous life (1 John 3:6–9). Those who practice wickedness, who plunge headlong into sin, who not only stumble but habitually walk in wickedness, should not be confident. This is no different from what Paul tells us in Romans 6, that we are no longer slaves to sin but slaves to righteousness, and in Galatians 5, that those who walk in the flesh will not inherit the kingdom. This is no different from what Jesus tells us in Matthew 7, that a good tree cannot bear bad fruit and a bad tree cannot bear good fruit. So if you live a morally righteous life, you should have confidence (1 John 3:24). And lest this standard make you despair, keep in mind that part of living a righteous life is refusing to claim that you live without sin and coming to Christ for cleansing when you do sin (1:9–10).

The third sign is social. You should have confidence if you love other Christians (1 John 3:14). If you hate like Cain, you do not have life. But if your heart and your wallet are open to your brothers and sisters, eternal life abides in you. One necessary sign of true spiritual life is that we love one another (4:7–12, 21).

These are John's three signposts to assure us that we are on the road that leads to eternal life. These are *not* three things we do to earn salvation, but three indicators that God has indeed saved us by his grace. We believe in Jesus Christ the Son of God. We live a righteous life. We are generous toward other Christians. Or we can put it this way: we know we have eternal life if we love Jesus, we love his commands, and we love his people. No one of the three is optional. All must be present in the Christian, and all three are meant to be signs for our assurance (see 1 John 2:4, 6; 4:20; 5:2).

A Tempest in a Blogspot

I've written thousands of blog posts over the years. Usually I have a pretty good idea of what people are going to love and what people are going to hate (it's almost always the same post that some people love and some people hate). But once in a while, even after nearly fifteen years of writing online, I'm surprised by what offends people. Case in point: the five paragraphs above. I wrote that same basic summary of 1 John on my blog several years ago, and some people *really* didn't like it. Here is one of the nicer criticisms:

As someone who's been struggling with [assurance] for some years, I am sorry to say this brief explanation can be so misleading. Not to be hateful. I follow your blog regularly and respect what you do. But who out there can confidently say they live without wickedness within or love their fellow "Christians" without fail?

This next comment was also respectful but voiced the same concern even more strongly:

I'm a little surprised and disappointed that Mr. DeYoung says nothing about faith in the finished work of Christ on the cross, and that he gives the appearance of leaning in the direction of trusting in one's own works for salvation, even if he does not intend to do so. While we do bear fruit, we bear it imperfectly, and we will always see our best works tainted with sinful actions or motivations. And Mr. DeYoung, as well intended as he may be, ultimately makes salvation rest on me and my efforts rather than on Christ and the cross.

Here was another thought along the same lines:

As a Christian who is currently stumbling and struggling, this article is pretty discouraging. I feel hopeless in the midst

WHO IS IT THAT OVERCOMES THE WORLD?

of my sin, and hopeless that I have failed to live a morally upright life, and I imagine myself knocking on heaven's gates one day and being denied entrance. Even though in my heart of hearts I know that I have encountered God's love and have known Him. . . . Can one so easily just look at the lack of moral uprightness in my life and say that I am not a Christian? Isn't this failure, this sin, the exact reason that I need Jesus and needed Him to give His life on the cross?

And here is one more comment, this time getting a bit more personal:

The problem with articles such as this is that definitive, objective answers are not provided. Nobody, not even Kevin DeYoung, lives a perfectly upright and moral life. While Kevin doesn't advocate sinless perfection here, it is very difficult to know if sin that you struggle with is part of your sanctification battle, or indication that you are making a practice of sin and are therefore not saved. . . . To the third point, absolutely we need to love others in the Body of Christ. But every person reading this, including the writer, loves his brothers and sisters imperfectly. If one is honest with themselves, they see this. How close to perfect must your love be before you have assurance of salvation?

Those were a few of the more substantive comments. One reader simply asked, "Is this the gospel? After all, this is the The Gospel Coalition website. What message are they preaching?" And perhaps summing up the concerns most succinctly, another reader advised: "TGC, please, it's time for a lengthy sit-down interview with Kevin. This is salvation we're talking about here."

Besides comments on the blog itself, a number of Christians wrote blog responses of their own. The criticisms centered on the same themes and issued from a certain way of thinking: "Look inside yourself, and what you'll find is that your heart is deceitful above all things. Look to your deeds, and you'll find that all your righteousness is as filthy rags. Look to your conscience, and you'll find that it testifies that nothing good dwells in you. If we rely on self-evaluation, all we'll get is the poison pill of doubt. Our hearts are not pure. Our deeds are not good. Our hands are not clean. The only possible way to get assurance is to look outside ourselves and trust in the finished work of Christ on our behalf."

I imagine many Christians resonate with that kind of response. But is it true? Or, more precisely, is it *all the way* true—not just accurate in what it means to affirm, but biblical in what it also denies?

Thou Dost Protest Too Much

Trying to distill the best arguments, I think there were three main objections to what I wrote on 1 John and assurance:

1. We should never look at ourselves for assurance.
2. We never really love God or love our neighbor.
3. This approach to assurance makes me doubt my salvation.

At the heart of all three objections is the assumption—more unstated than argued from Scripture—that living an obedient Christian life is not possible, that the only two options before us are trusting in our own works for salvation or admitting to unrelenting spiritual failure. If, however, those two options present us with a false dilemma, then the three objections fall away.

Let's look at each one in turn.

Objection #1: We Should Never Look at Ourselves for Assurance

From the outset, we should remember that the three signs (theological, moral, and social) in 1 John are just that, signs. These are not three things we do to earn salvation but three indicators that God has indeed saved us. When driving across country, the road signs don't fuel your car or drive it for you or move you from point A to point B. The signs let you know that you are going in the right direction. There is no works righteousness here. That would contradict 1 John 1:8 (we all still sin) and 1 John 2:1–2 (we need an advocate and a propitiatory sacrifice), not to mention the rest of the Bible. The three exhortations—love Jesus, love his commands, and love your neighbor—are not instructions for building a ladder to heaven. They are three kinds of fruit that can be plucked from the tree of your life when you are a genuine born-again Christian.

It sounds spiritual to suppose that we can never gain any confidence about our spiritual condition except by looking to Christ. But that ignores the actual argument of John's epistle. First John was written so that we might know something, that we might see, that we might discern truth from error by looking at people's lives—what they do, what they believe, and how they act:

- 1 John 2:5–6: "By this we may know that we are in him." And how do you know if you are in him? Answer: "Whoever says he abides in him ought to walk in the same way in which he walked." That's how we know.

- 1 John 3:10: "By this it is evident who are the children of God, and who are the children of the devil." And what is this evidence? "Whoever does not practice righteousness is not of God, nor is the one who does not love his brother."

- 1 John 3:14: "We know that we have passed out of death into life." And how do we know that? "Because we love the brothers."

- 1 John 3:19: "By this we shall know that we are of the truth and reassure our heart before him," and 1 John 3:24: "Whoever keeps his commandments abides in God, and God in him. And by this we know that he abides in us."

Over and over in 1 John we are told, "By this we know . . ." We are meant to see something and conclude something based on our lives.

The trouble—that we bring upon ourselves, not that the Bible forces upon us—is that we assume it is the better part of piety to always conclude that we are not keeping God's commands. We think true humility requires us to assess ourselves negatively in every respect. When Paul tells the Corinthians, "Examine yourselves, to see whether you are in the faith" (2 Cor. 13:5), we often miss the larger point. Paul wanted them to remember that he was a legitimate minister of Christ because he was their father in the faith. The Corinthian believers were the seal of his apostleship. Paul told them to examine themselves because he expected the Corinthians to give themselves a passing grade on the test.

Looking at fruit in our lives is not the *only* means by which we grow in assurance, but it is *one* of the means. The Reformed confessions are consistent on this point. The Canons of Dort, for example, explain that assurance springs from three sources: "from faith in God's promises, which He has most abundantly revealed in His Word for our comfort; from the testimony of the Holy Spirit, witnessing with our spirit that we are children and heirs of God; and lastly, from a serious and holy desire to preserve a good conscience and perform good works" (CD 5.10). The Westminster Confession of Faith says the same thing. The "infallible assurance of faith" is "founded upon the divine truth of the promises of salvation, the inward evidence of those graces . . . [and] the testimony of the Spirit of adoption" (WCF 18.2). The Reformed confessions teach that a transformed life is one sign of our union with Christ—not the only sign and not the ground of our right standing with God, but one important indicator that we are truly born again.

If grace has come to us, we should expect to see grace flowing out of us. We may have seasons of doubt (Jude 22).

We may struggle to do the right thing (Rom. 7:18–20). The Westminster Confession fully recognizes that infallible assurance does not belong to the essence of faith (18.3) and that believers can have their confidence shaken (18.4), but the goal is to live life assured they are in a state of grace (18.1).

Let's go back to the second sign from the Westminster Confession ("inward evidence of those graces"). The confession lists four proof texts:

- 2 Peter 1:4–11, which urges us to make our calling and election sure by the diligent effort to grow in godliness and bear spiritual fruit;
- 1 John 2:3, which testifies that we know we belong to God if we keep his commandments;
- 1 John 3:14, which assures us that we have passed from death to life because we love our brothers;
- 2 Corinthians 1:12, which speaks of rejoicing in the testimony of a good conscience.

These verses remind us that opening our eyes to evidences of grace is not the same as earning our salvation or thinking we have reached perfection. Christians are meant to be confident (1 John 3:21). Our consciences are supposed to be clean

(Acts 24:16; 1 Tim. 1:19). We have permission to examine ourselves and pass the test.

Objection #2: We Never Really Love God or Love Our Neighbor

Of course, we can make this objection a true statement, if we mean perfect love and flawless obedience. But if love and obedience must always be understood as perfect and flawless, we won't be able to take the Bible on its own terms. "By this we know that we love the children of God, when we love God and obey his commandments" (1 John 5:2). Surely this is not an empty set. John is not speaking hypothetically. He believes there are people who genuinely love God and obey his commandments.

Look at this remarkable statement in verse 4: "For everyone who has been born of God overcomes the world." If you struggle with temptations and fears and doubts and sins, that is the normal pattern of the Christian life. But if you eagerly jump into sin, do not turn from sin, your life is habitually marked by sin, and you revel in sin, then you are at odds with what Scripture tells us to do and expects us to be as Christians. Three times in verses 4 and 5 John speaks of overcoming. Are Christians weak? Yes, in terms of humility, dependence, suffering, lack of self-regard, and lack of impressive credentials (2 Cor. 12:1–10). But Christians are not to be "weak" if weakness means a life mired in unchecked sin and spiritual failure. Christians are conquerors, not capitulators; overcomers, not succumbers (cf. Rev. 2:7, 11, 17, 26; 3:5, 12, 21).

Too many Christians make the mistake of thinking that if they are to be seriously godly, they must utterly denigrate everything they do as Christians. To be sure, we cannot fulfill the law absolutely. The Westminster Confession reminds us that Christians still "fall short of much which in duty they are bound to do" (WCF 16.4). Even our best works "are defiled, and mixed with so much weakness and imperfection, that they cannot endure the severity of God's judgment" (WCF 16.5). And yet, the confession continues, our good works are accepted in Christ, not because they are wholly unblameable, but because, in view of the Son's work, God "is pleased to accept and reward that which is sincere, although accompanied with many weaknesses and imperfections" (WCF 16.6). In other words, Christ died to expiate our evil deeds *and* to cleanse our good works. God looks on us *and* our works and sees both as better than we deserve.

Here is where the careful distinctions of scholastic theology are necessary. "We must distinguish," writes Francis Turretin, "between truly good and perfectly good." The latter category "cannot be ascribed to the works of the saints on account of the imperfection of sanctification and the remains of sin." But the former category "is rightly predicated of them because though they are not as yet perfectly renewed, still they are truly good and unfeignedly renewed."[2]

According to Turretin, there are at least three reasons why we must conclude that the works of believers can be truly good.[3] First, our good works are performed by a special motion and impulse of the Holy Spirit. Second, Scripture repeatedly says that such works please God. And third, the saints are promised a reward for their good works. If, in order to sound extra pious and humble, we insist that our good works are actually nothing of the sort, we end up making too little of the Spirit's work in our lives and muting dozens of biblical texts. While it may be true that even our best deeds are still sinful, in the sense that they are still not perfectly righteous, the nature of our good works is still good.

Simply put, the good works of believers can be truly good works, even if the mode in which they are done is imperfect. When Jeremiah lamented that "the heart is deceitful above all things, and desperately sick" (Jer. 17:9), he was chiding Judah for its rank rebellion, not making a judgment on the

2 Francis Turretin, *Institutes of Elenctic Theology*, 3 vols., trans. George Musgrave Giger, ed. James T. Dennison Jr. (Phillipsburg, NJ: P&R, 1997), 2:708.
3 Turretin, *Institutes*, 2:708–9.

potential obedience of born-again Christians. Likewise, Isaiah's famous statement that "all our righteous deeds are like a polluted garment" (Isa. 64:6) was an indictment of perfunctory, heartless obedience (65:7), not a refusal to acknowledge that God's people can ever do what is righteous. The verse *right before* the "polluted garment" verse says about God: "You meet him who joyfully works righteousness, those who remember you in your ways" (64:5). Obedience is a real category; doing what is right is not impossible.

Objection #3: This Approach to Assurance Makes Me Doubt My Salvation

This is the most personal and pastoral objection. There are some who should doubt, but not those who desire holiness, hate their sin, and flee to Christ. The book of 1 John is not meant to make us doubt. It is meant to make us discerning, and through discernment to have confidence. John's letter was meant to help those who are children of our heavenly Father. That's why John addresses them as little children (1 John 2:12, 28; 3:1; 5:21). "There are false teachers out there," John says. "Don't listen to them. Don't run after sin. Trust in Christ. Walk with Christ. I want you to be confident in your position in Christ. Then your joy will be filled to overflowing."

To those who ask, "How do I know if I am loving enough?" let me give you three words: *trajectory*, *community*, and *apology*.

Trajectory. Don't measure how you're doing today compared to two days ago but look over months and years. Is there growth in godliness? Is there love for the things of God? Look for a long-term pattern. And remember, this trajectory is not how you get saved, but one indication that you are saved.

Community. Assurance is a community project. The closer you get to a holy God, the more you see your own sin. We need other people to point out fruit in our lives. We need the church to discern that we are genuine members of the body of Christ. Don't spend all your time peeling back the onion layers of your soul. Entrust yourself to godly elders and good spiritual friends.

Apology. Cultivate a life of repentance. One of the signs that you are walking in the light is that you are honest about having walked in the darkness. This doesn't mean you do not sin anymore or that you still do not have some dark times. It means that you bring your sin into the light and are honest about it, turn from it, and run to Christ.

Born-again Christians are changed Christians. The change will be stumbling, imperfect, and full of temptation and struggle, but the change is nevertheless real, sincere, and discernible. This is not about pride. This is about believing that the amazing grace that saves a wretch like me is the same grace that leads us home. Let us not minimize the work of Christ by making him half a Savior—strong enough to save us from our sins but not strong enough to transform our sin-stained lives.

It is the new birth that makes this life of obedience possible—not because you woke up one morning and thought you would become a Christian, and then you tried really hard to get your life together. It is by God's sovereign work of grace that you have new life and a new spirit and a new heart. When a woman has a baby, the baby is the evidence of the new life. If you never saw the baby, you would wonder if she had really given birth. So why is it automatically prideful to recognize evidence of your spiritual new birth? It is not boasting to say, "I worked harder than any of them," if you then say, "though it was not I, but the grace of God that is with me" (1 Cor. 15:10). It is not vanity to think that, by God's regenerating and sustaining grace, we who believe Jesus is the Son of God are those who overcome the world (1 John 5:5).

3

Never Enough

I CONFESS I'VE NEVER seen the movie all the way through, but *The Greatest Showman* has been on plenty of times in my house. I've only caught bits and pieces, so I'm not really sure what the story is about, but Wolverine runs a circus or something, and Ilsa Faust from MI6 is there, and so is Spider-Man's girlfriend. Anyway, there is a moving song at some point called "Never Enough."[4] I think the *Mission: Impossible* lady pretends to sing it. You've probably gotten the song stuck in your head for a day or two or three years. It's very catchy, sung with lots of energy and emotion. My wife and I often break into "Never Enough" when the kids want

---

4   Loren Allred, "Never Enough," in *The Greatest Showman*, directed by Michael Gracey (Los Angeles: 20th Century Studios, 2017).

a third bowl of cereal at bedtime, or they can't live without another sleepover, or one of them collapses in tears of disappointment by Christmas afternoon.

The song is certainly true when it comes to childhood desires and the insatiable appetite many adults have for fame and fortune. But what about God? We've already established that we can't earn our way into heaven and that our best deeds as Christians are imperfect. But does that mean that every effort at heartfelt obedience is never enough for our heavenly Father? Are we doomed to spend our Christian lives like Sisyphus, pushing the immense boulder of God's expectations up a giant hill, only to have the rock roll back down the hill in endless futility? When we sign up to follow Jesus, are we signing up for a lifetime of frustration and disappointment—not just our frustration with the demands of Christianity, but God's disappointment with us?

Over the next few chapters I want to look at several areas of the Christian life where we are especially prone to feeling like we are never enough. We will examine what the Bible says about money, what the Bible says about corporate guilt, and what the Bible says about repairing a broken planet. That's where we are going in the chapters ahead. In this chapter I want to deal with two other areas of Christianity—two aspects of the Christian life that we all know we should do, and we all want to do better. These are two habits of Discipleship 101. Most of us have heard (or given) countless sermons and talks on these two subjects. I'm talking about prayer and evangelism, or to put it in the vernacular, having a daily quiet time and sharing our faith.

The Quest for More Quiet Time

I already feel nervous starting this section. I'd hate for someone to walk away from this chapter thinking, "Wow, I love this book. No more daily prayer and Bible reading!" Let me be clear: that is *not* the point of this chapter. As we will see in a moment, the Bible does tell us to pray. The Bible also presumes that God's people will be intimately familiar with the Scriptures and pass along its truths to their children. Meet any mature, fruitful Christian, and you can almost guarantee he regularly has something like a "quiet time"—a time set aside to talk to God in prayer and hear from God in the word.

I am not anti–quiet time or anti–daily devotions or anti–family worship. All of these disciplines serve God's people well and have been around for a long time. What does not serve God's people well is the unstated (and sometimes stated) assumption—put upon us by others or by ourselves—that Christianity is only for super-disciplined neatniks who get up before dawn, redeem every minute of the day, and have very organized sock drawers. Spiritual disciplines are great (and necessary) when the goal is to know God better. Spiritual disciplines are soul-crushing when the aim is to get our metaphysical workout in each day, knowing that we could always exercise more if we were better Christians.

I first began my habit of daily devotions when I was in high school. A couple of my friends at school were serious Christians, and they talked about spending time in their Bibles every morning before school. That wasn't something I was doing at the time, but it sounded like a good idea. My motives were somewhat mixed. I was motivated to pray every day that God would bless my running and that I would meet my goal of being all-county JV (like I said, I can be the best of the second tier or the worst of the pretty good). I spent a few minutes in prayer each day, and read one chapter in the Bible along with a daily reading from a simple devotional book. It took only 5 to 10 minutes, but it was a massive catalyst in helping me grow as a Christian.

Once in college, my faith grew like a weed—which is the right phrase, because although there was a lot of good going on in my spiritual life, there were also species of pride growing up at the same time. I was especially fastidious about my quiet time. I almost never missed a day, sometimes trudging through snow to get to my school's prayer chapel, often fighting to stay awake during prayer because I was a college student after all, and I stayed up way too late. Many of my quiet times ended up really quiet! Nevertheless, I read through the Bible several times. I kept a prayer journal. I was, compared to most of my peers, a quiet-time champion. But I also felt terrible if I ever missed a day. I knew intellectually that I wasn't earning God's favor, but in my heart it felt like I was only a good Christian once I read my chapters and prayed my prayers. Looking back, I can see that the Lord used my zeal in many good ways. I can also see that there were more obvious biblical commands that I neglected so long as the quiet-time box was checked every morning.

This prompts an important question: Do the Scriptures command a daily devotional time of prayer and Bible reading? Not exactly, but they presume something like it. On the one hand, we must be honest with what we do and do not see in the Bible. Family worship is not one of the Ten Commandments. Jesus did not outline M'Cheyne's Bible reading plan in the Sermon on the Mount. The vice lists in the New Testament do not mention "delinquent in devotions," and "crushes his quiet time every morning" is not listed among the fruit of the Spirit. We must be careful not to make the minutes (or hours) we spend in daily devotions the sine qua non of Christian discipleship. Too many of us have learned to measure our discipleship according to this one criterion, and because we can always spend more time in prayer, we never seem to be measuring up.

And yet if that's all we said about "having a quiet time"—it's nowhere commanded in Scripture—we would not be telling the whole story. We are often commanded to pray (Matt. 7:7–11; Rom. 12:12; 1 Thess. 5:17). Jesus assumes that God's people will often be in private prayer (Matt. 6:6) and that the habit of prayer will be daily (Matt. 6:11). We know that Jesus withdrew to desolate places to pray (Mark 1:35) and that godly men like Daniel prayed three times a day (Dan. 6:10). Likewise, the Psalms commend to us the habit of meditating on God's word day and night (Pss. 1; 119). We see in Timothy the example of public and private reading of Scripture (1 Tim. 4:13, 15; 2 Tim. 3:15). And, finally, on a number of occasions the Bible exhorts parents, and especially fathers, to instruct their children in the way of the Lord (Gen. 18:19; Deut. 6:5–6; Ps. 78:4; Eph. 6:4). There is no way to be faithful to these scriptural commands and examples if our lives are devoid of prayer, Bible reading, and time with our families in the word.

So are we right back where we started, with a crushing sense that we can never spend enough time in private and family worship? I hope not. Notice that while the Bible says a lot about the *what*—be devoted to prayer, meditate on God's law, teach your children—it does not say a lot about the *how*. Developing personal spiritual disciplines is one way to the *what*, but there are many others: corporate worship, small-group Bible studies, listening to sermons in the car, listening to the Bible while you walk, listening to Bible teaching while you do the dishes, Christian schools, Christian books, spiritual conversations, prayers before meals, prayers at bedtime, and prayers over the phone.

So, yes, we should cultivate the habit of prayer and Bible reading, but we should not think that God puts impossible standards upon us as frail, finite creatures. When the disciples implored Jesus, "Lord, teach us to pray" (Luke 11:1), Jesus didn't give them specifics about time, place, position, and duration. He taught them what to say. Praying for the right reasons (not to be seen by others), to the right person (our heavenly Father), with the right petitions (hallowed be your name, your kingdom come, your will be done, give, forgive, protect) is far more important than the discipline meant to enable our prayers.

If I'm not mistaken, my wife likes to spend time with me. She likes talking to me and having me talk to her. When I'm overly busy, she won't hesitate to ask for more of my attention. And even as a selfish husband, I'm usually eager to oblige because I love my wife. I love to spend time with her. Even after more than twenty years, there are still plenty of things to do and talk about. But because our lives are hectic and full, getting time together often requires planning and intentionality. If my wife made me check in every day at a set time, kept track of how many minutes I talked to her, and then rolled her eyes whenever I did anything else besides talk to her, that would make for a miserable marriage. But if I never made an effort to get a babysitter, go on a walk with her, plan a getaway, or simply put down my phone and look her in the eye, our marriage would likely grow stale and distant.

Will there always be more I can do to become a better husband? Of course. But that doesn't mean I can't be a genuinely good husband or that my wife can't be happy with our marriage. One of the saddest things in a marriage is when one or both spouses are impossible to please, when good-faith efforts are never enough, when past hurts are never forgotten, when imperfections are always put front and center. Happy marriages are different. They require work. They don't happen by accident. But they are possible. That's what our relationship with God is like as well. Following Jesus takes time and effort, but we don't have to be time-management gurus or monastic ascetics to walk with him in faithfulness and fruitfulness.

Is Christianity Only for Extroverts?

If our notion of a "quiet time" is hinted at here and there in the Bible but never explicitly commanded, popular notions of personal evangelism are even less well-attested in Scripture. Again, let me hasten to add that sharing the gospel with non-Christians is necessary work, and most Christians and most churches would do well to grow in courage for this ministry. But for all the emphasis we put on personal evangelism—sometimes treating it as *the* good work above all other good works—there are few verses we can go to in order to underscore its importance. There are verses directed to pastors and church officers to preach the word (2 Tim. 4:1–2) and do the work of an evangelist (4:5). There are verses about sending preachers out with the gospel so that people might believe and be saved (Rom. 10:14–15). There are verses about God's plan to redeem people from every tribe, language, and nation (Gen. 12:1–3; Matt. 28:19–20; Rev. 5:9–10; 7:9–10). There is an entire book of the Bible (Acts) about the apostolic mission to evangelize the lost, disciple new converts, and plant strong churches (see Acts 14:21–23). What we don't have are a lot of verses commanding individual Christians to share their faith.

Of course, just as we saw with "quiet times," if we stopped here, we would not get the whole story. Peter exhorts us to be ready to make a defense and to give a reason for the hope we have (1 Pet. 3:15). Similarly, the armor of God in Ephesians 6 includes shoes that equip us with a "readiness given by the gospel of peace" (v. 15). We see evidence that the Corinthians were to be concerned for the salvation of nonbelievers (1 Cor. 7:12–16; 14:23–25) and that Titus was to instruct God's people to adorn with their faith and obedience the doctrine of God our Savior (Titus 2:10). More clearly, we see evangelistic activity at work in the Thessalonian church where the word was at work in the believers (1 Thess. 2:13–16), the word was running ahead (2 Thess. 3:1), and the word was ringing and sounding forth (1 Thess. 1:8).

And what about the Great Commission? No doubt this is the lodestar text for most Christians when it comes to our evangelistic obligations. We are all told—right there in black and white—to make disciples. Or are we? The commission in Matthew's Gospel is given explicitly to the eleven remaining apostles (Matt. 28:16–18). While we are right to understand the commission as being for us in some way (hence the promise to be with them to "the end of the age"), we must also admit that there are specific instructions we don't all follow. We are not waiting in Jerusalem for the outpouring of the Holy Spirit (see Luke 24:49; Acts 1:4), and not many of us will literally bear witness in Jerusalem or Judea or Samaria (see Acts 1:8). Most Christians do not "go" as Matthew 28:19 commands, nor do most Christians perform baptisms. We understand instinctively that the Great Commission is ours by application more than by direct command.

This is an important point. The Great Commission was, first, for the apostles and then, by extension, for the church they would leave behind. This means that the Great Commission is our mission not as a personal job description but insofar as we are members of Christ's church. The mission of the church is the Great Commission. Therefore, we all have a role to play and ought to have an earnest desire in seeing that mission accomplished. None of us are literal apostles. Some of us are ordained preachers. Others are sent-out missionaries. All of us can give and pray and labor to see our churches engaged in the Great Commission.

We have to acknowledge what we see and don't see in the Bible. On the one hand, we see that the word preached to the church should not just stay in the church but flow through the church to outsiders. On the other hand, there is no indication that every conversation must turn to the gospel, or that our vocations can only be justified if we share our faith regularly, or that evangelism should trump all other ecclesiastical and doctrinal concerns. The New Testament encourages us to be ready to explain our Christian faith when asked; it encourages us to make the gospel look attractive by our honest and obedient lives; it encourages us to be concerned for the salvation of the lost; it encourages preachers to be faithful in teaching the gospel; it encourages believers to be conduits for the word of God. The New Testament does not expect us all to be extroverts, gifted conversationalists, and cold-call evangelists.

I know that one of the chief objections to Reformed soteriology is the assumption that if Christians believe in unconditional election, then they won't evangelize. That's not how Paul reasoned from Romans 9 ("he has mercy on whomever he wills," v. 18) to Romans 10 ("my heart's desire and prayer to God for them is that they may be saved," v. 1), and that's not how famous Calvinists like George Whitefield, Jonathan Edwards, or William Carey preached the word or lived their lives. At the same time, we need a firm belief in God's sovereignty in salvation, lest we think everything—or, in an ultimate sense, *anything*—depends on us. God never meant for evangelism to be the single defining characteristic of faithful Christianity. When personal evangelism becomes more central than dozens of more explicit commands, we are not only tempted to compromise on doctrinal and missiological integrity; we become weighed down by the impossibility of the task. There are always more people to speak to, always more conversations we could have, always more lost people to reach. The "never enough" never lets up.

Part of the problem is the way many pastors talk about these things. As a preacher, I know how to deliver a sermon so that everyone feels convicted. It's tempting to think that every good sermon leaves every Christian feeling guilty for something. So every sermon about holiness leaves everyone feeling unholy. Every sermon on prayer makes people feel guilty for not praying more. Every sermon on evangelism causes the whole congregation to squirm in supposed disobedience. That's not healthy preaching, and it doesn't make for healthy congregations. After more than twenty years in pastoral ministry, I now make a point to tell people in my sermons, "Many of you are being faithful in prayer." "I see marks of godliness in most of you." "Some of you are great examples of sharing your faith." Too often, pastors preach what they don't really mean. They don't *really* think everyone is failing in every way, but they've learned to preach that way because it feels powerful and, truth be told, some people like it. As a result, God's people are trained to conclude that because they could always do more (of some good discipline or practice), they are not doing enough.

God has not made us all in the same way, and he does not expect the word to flow through us all in the same way. You may end up being a preacher or a missionary. You may learn to love beach evangelism, handing out tracts, and knocking on doors. You may have gifts to easily converse with strangers. Or your gifts may be in hospitality. Or in writing. Or in public debates. Or you may be the beloved neighbor who gets the opportunity to speak of Jesus because you represent him so well. God wants us to have a heart for the lost. He wants us to further the church's overall mission in reaching the nations. He wants us to be ready to walk through open doors. But he never says that personal evangelism is what the Christian life is all about. Saving sinners is the impossible part; God does that. Our part is to ensure—in whatever way God has shaped us and in whatever opportunities he gives us—that the gospel that has come to us also flows out of us. Some Christians would make good salespeople; all good Christians are happy to talk about Jesus.

4

The Camel in the Room

I CAN'T FIND WHERE (or if) G. K. Chesterton really said it, but I've seen it attributed to Chesterton often, and it sure does sound like him:

> It may be possible to have a good debate over whether or not Jesus believed in fairies. It is a tantalizing question. Alas, it is impossible to have any sort of debate over whether or not Jesus believed that rich people were in big trouble—there is too much evidence on the subject, and it is overwhelming.

Strikes me as Chestertonian in character. And *partially* true. There are big dangers associated with being rich. Jesus makes that point pretty clear. But if there are big dangers for the rich, there are also big opportunities. One of the chief "never enough" areas of Christian discipleship relates to Christians and their money. Let's be honest: many of us are rich—certainly rich compared to most people throughout human history, probably rich compared to most people in the world, and possibly rich even by the standards of Western prosperity. We need to talk about the camel in the room—as in, can it really get through the eye of a needle?

While there are plenty of denunciations of rich oppressors and a myriad of texts that warn us against the temptations associated with wealth, the Bible is not antirich. Abraham and Job were rich. So were the good kings of Israel and Judah. So were some of the first disciples. The parables of Jesus often commend people for being shrewd with their money, and the reward for being a good steward of a little is often being entrusted with even more. The Bible is emphatically against the normal way rich people view and use their money. The Bible is not against wealth and possessions as such. Rich people should not despair of ever being faithful followers of Jesus.

Evangelist to the Rich

Anyone who has studied the Gospels knows that Luke's Gospel uses the harshest language toward the rich and includes the most about our obligations to the poor. For example, in

Luke's version of the Beatitudes, Jesus not only pronounces a blessing on the poor (Luke 6:20); he also pronounces curses on the rich. "Woe to you who are rich, for you have received your consolation. Woe to you who are full now, for you shall be hungry" (Luke 6:24–25). Of the four Gospel writers Luke has the most to say about wealth and poverty. He chooses his material and organizes it in such a way that his audience would understand that how you handle your money has everything to do with following Jesus.

With this obvious emphasis, it's easy to make Luke (and the Jesus he writes about) into someone vigorously opposed to rich people. Indeed, many Christians look immediately to Luke when they want to say something "prophetic" against materialism or income disparity or the wealth of the Western world. While these "prophetic" words are sometimes necessary, they don't do justice to Luke's aims and appeals. We make a profound mistake to see Luke as an evangelist *against* the rich. He is, more accurately, an evangelist *to* the rich.

We must remember two things if we are going to understand Luke's attitude toward wealth and poverty.

First, Luke was almost certainly writing to the rich. Both of his books are addressed to Theophilus (Luke 1:3; Acts 1:1). In his Gospel, Luke gives Theophilus the title "most excellent," the same honorific given to the Roman magistrates Felix

(Acts 23:26) and Festus (Acts 26:25). Most scholars figure that Theophilus was some kind of Roman official, or at least a person of some social standing, who was recently converted and in need of firm grounding in the faith.

Second, Luke was most likely relatively well-off himself. This occasional traveler with Paul was known as "the beloved physician" (Col. 4:14), not a meager profession now or then. Moreover, Luke shows evidence in his writing of being well-educated, well-traveled, and well-connected—a cosmopolitan Gentile convert and probably a person of some means.

Luke was not a poor man writing to poor people that together they might denounce the rich. It's much closer to the truth to say Luke was a rich man writing to another rich man (and people like him) in order to show how the rich could truly follow Jesus.

This thesis statement may sound strange, even jarring, but when we look closer at Luke's Gospel and then at Acts we see several instances—unique to Luke—of rich people "getting it" and using their money well. Luke includes much material to warn and rebuke the rich. He also includes a surprising number of examples of wealthy persons who demonstrate genuine discipleship of Christ.

A brief survey of the relevant material in Luke-Acts will bear out both these points. Luke, more than any other biblical writer, wants us to see that the rich often get it wrong, but they can also get it right.

Rich and Poor in Luke

We read in Mary's Magnificat about the great reversal that is coming where the poor will be exalted and the rich will be cast down (Luke 1:51–53). From the outset of the Gospel, we see that the humble, hungry, and poor are in a position of future blessing, while the proud, exalted, and rich are in danger.

In Luke 3 John the Baptist explains that repentance is directly tied to what you do with your money (vv. 10–14). Importantly, however, the text never suggests that being a tax collector or a solider made one complicit in an oppressive Roman regime. One could make money and work for the Romans without automatically being guilty of Rome's sins and injustices.

We see Jesus preaching in his hometown of Nazareth in Luke 4. He reads from Isaiah 61 and identifies himself as the Spirit-anointed prophet sent to preach good news to the poor (4:18). In what follows, Jesus gives two examples of the "poor" who received the good news. He mentions the widow of Zarephath (4:25–26), who was materially poor. And then he mentions Naaman the Syrian general (4:27), who was materially rich. Here is our first example of a rich man who "got it." Though he was an elite general, Naaman was humble enough to seek Elisha's help and dip himself in the Jordan River.

In Luke 5 we see Jesus calling a tax collector named Levi to follow him. And when Levi followed Jesus, he left everything behind and then later threw a big party in his house with all sorts of tax collectors (5:27–29). Here, then, is another rich man doing the right thing. He left his profession behind (at least for the moment), but he does not seem to have left all his wealth behind.

In Luke 8 we see a number of rich women serving as patrons for Jesus's ministry and for his disciples (vv. 2–3). More rich people using their money well.

In Luke 10 we meet the good Samaritan who is justly famous for stopping to help the needy man on the side of the road. Here we also see negative examples of the societal elite ignoring urgent needs right in front of them.

In Luke 12 we meet the rich fool who lives for himself and trusts in his wealth to save him on the last day (vv. 15, 20–21). If you are a rich man depending on your riches, you are (as the kids would say) not doing it right.

In Luke 14 the kingdom is compared to a wedding feast and then to a great banquet. Austerity and asceticism, while necessary at times, are not pictures of the good life God has waiting for his people.

In Luke 15 we see the prodigal son waste his inheritance on wild living, only to come to his senses when he is poor and destitute. Again, Luke (and Jesus) shows us the danger of wealth and the blessing that can come from being poor. But we also see another example of a wide-hearted rich man. The prodigal's father threw caution to the wind and spread a feast for his long-lost son.

In Luke 16 we have an example of a rich man using his wealth wisely and an example of a rich man using his wealth poorly. First, we have the parable of the dishonest manager. Don't get hung up on the fact that Jesus is using a bad man to be a good example. The larger point is clear enough: be shrewd with your money and faithful with your earthly wealth so that you can do strategic heavenly good (16:8–9). Second, we have the story of the rich man and Lazarus. This is the negative example to contrast with the positive example earlier in the chapter. The rich man lived in self-satisfied luxury and ignored the needs right in front of him (16:19–21). He must suffer ceaseless torment in the flames of judgment.

The book ends with a positive example, as Joseph of Ari-mathea, a member of the council, "a good and righteous man," does not consent to the council's decision and asks Pilate for the body of Jesus (Luke 23:50–53). This was just as the prophet Isaiah predicted, that the suffering servant would be buried with a rich man in his death (Isa. 53:9).

So, what have we seen in Luke's Gospel? We've seen that the rich face unique dangers. They can be callous toward others, haughty, proud, cheats, swindlers, wrongly confident in themselves, and foolishly trusting in their wealth. If that is your life now, Luke says, you are in for a rude awakening at the end of the age, because everything will be turned upside down. The humble poor will be lifted up; the arrogant rich will be cast down.

On the other hand, we also see how the rich can be faithful with their wealth. The rich support Jesus and his ministry. They stand up for what is right. They use their money wisely for spiritual gain. The righteous rich in Luke are still rich, but they are also generous, repentant of any wrongs, and faithful to the cause of Christ.

Rich and Poor in Acts

In the book of Acts, just as in Luke, we see both kinds of examples. We see rich people at their worst, and we see how rich people can inherit the kingdom of God and live out its values.

Believers in the early church had everything in common (Acts 2:44; 4:32). At first glance it can look like the church modeled an early form of communism, and many have tried to use the text in that way. They see it reminiscent of the Marxist slogan, "From each according to his ability; to each according to his need." In fact, later in Acts 11:29 we read, "So the disciples determined, every one according to his ability, to send relief to the brothers living in Judea." But two realities distinguish sharing in the early church from communism.

First, they did not abolish private property (see Acts 4:34, 37; 5:4). People still owned their homes (e.g., Lydia, house churches, Mary the mother of John Mark). Businesses were not collectivized. The state did not own the land. Each one who owned property was free to do with it as he saw fit.

Second, the selling and distribution of their possessions was not by force or coercion but free and voluntary. The church had a wonderful communal spirit, but that is far different from the spirit of state-enforced communism. The expression "everything in common" was used to describe the radical generosity of the early church. Their pattern is a model for God's people. The church was fulfilling the ideal of the promised land, in which "there will be no poor among you" (Deut. 15:4). Radical generosity in the church is a sign of the in-breaking of the kingdom. When we share with our brothers and sisters in need, we demonstrate that God's promised reign and rule is taking root here and now. It's a little bit of heaven on earth.

In Acts 8 we see Simon trying to buy the power of the Spirit with money (vv. 14–24). Peter tells him, "May your silver perish with you" (8:20). This is where we get the word *simony*, which was prevalent in the Middle Ages; it means the buying of church offices. This is an example of the unrighteous rich.

Dorcas in Acts 9 is the opposite example, as she is said to be full of good works and acts of charity (vv. 36–37).

Lydia was likely a wealthy woman. She was a seller of purple goods (high-end retail clothing at the time) and had a house in which to host Paul and his companions (Acts 16:11–15). This rich person "gets it."

The next story is of a rich person who doesn't "get it." A slave girl was used to make money for her owners by fortune-telling. When Paul delivered her from the spirit that inhabited her, the owners got upset because their gravy train was about to fall off the tracks. So they used their connections to haul Paul and Silas before the rulers of the city, who then gave the order for them to be beaten with rods (Acts 16:16–24). More rich people blinded by their wealth.

In Acts 17 we are told that many leading women of the city believed (vv. 4, 12). More rich people turning to Christ.

In Acts 19 we see that when many people were converted in Ephesus, they began divulging their pagan practices. They burned their magic books, and the value came out to fifty thousand pieces of silver. They renounced their former vocation, and its lucrative practice, in coming to Christ (19:18–19). Rich people repenting of unrighteous mammon.

Right after this positive example, we have another negative example. Demetrius, a silversmith in Ephesus, was upset that Paul was ruining his business of making gods and goddesses (Acts 19:24–27). People were so angry that their religious and economic way of life was being threatened that a riot broke out in the city (19:28–29).

Wretched Rich and Righteous Rich

We have seen in Luke-Acts a number of these pairings: rich people making an idol of wealth *and* rich people demonstrating a transformed attitude toward wealth.

We have the shrewd manager and then the rich man and Lazarus in Luke 16.

We have in Acts 16 the example of Lydia, a rich person who gets it, and then the rich owners of the slave girl, who don't get it.

And in Acts 19 we see some in Ephesus who give up their magic arts at great financial cost to themselves, and then we see others in Ephesus who cause a riot because they've gotten rich from making idols, and the gospel is threatening their way of life.

These pairings strongly suggest that Luke was trying to show Theophilus how he, as a rich member of the elite class, could sincerely and obediently follow Christ.

If you aren't convinced by this thesis, let me go back to two obvious pairings I skipped over. These are the most important wretched rich/righteous rich pairings in Luke-Acts. We find one in each book.

We meet two of the most famous rich people in the Bible in Luke 18 and 19. First we have the rich ruler who hears what Jesus says about money and becomes sad because he thought he was a good person until he realized that following Jesus was going to affect his bank account (Luke 18:24–25). For a moment it looks like it's impossible for a rich man to be saved. If possible at all, it seems to require giving away everything. But Jesus holds out hope that what is impossible with man is possible with God (18:27).

The question—"Then who can be saved?" (Luke 18:26)—is answered in the next chapter when we meet Zacchaeus, a rich man who demonstrates his conversion by showing an entirely new attitude toward money (19:8). Zacchaeus didn't literally give away everything he owned (like Jesus demanded of the rich ruler in 18:22), but Zacchaeus is clearly a changed man. He realizes that following Jesus means repenting of his cheating ways. Zacchaeus does not trade places with the poor, but he turns from his wickedness and turns to Christ with a new heart of obedience and generosity.

The other obvious pairing is in Acts 4 and 5, where we find the deliberate contrast between Barnabas, a rich man who "gets it," and Ananias and Sapphira as rich people just going through the motions.

Barnabas was a native of Cyprus and a Levite (the prohibition of owning land must have fallen by the wayside). As a Levite, he was likely part of the social elite. As a landowner he was part of the upper crust in Judea. Maybe as few as 5 percent of the Jews owned land. Barnabas sold a field and brought the money to the apostles to distribute. (Interesting that Luke doesn't mind telling us who gave this gift. Maybe it was already obvious. Or maybe sometimes it's appropriate to point out examples of giving just like we might point out examples in the areas of evangelism or prayer.) Here then was a rich member of the elite who modeled Spirit-prompted generosity.

Then in the next chapter we read of two more rich people, Ananias and Sapphira. They too sold a piece of property and laid the money at the apostles' feet (Acts 5:1–2). But they lied about how much they were giving. They kept some of the proceeds for themselves, which would have been perfectly fine, except that they lied about it so they could look as impressive as Barnabas. God killed them both for their deception (5:5–10). They are the negative foil to Barnabas's commendable behavior.

Over and over, then, Luke is communicating to rich people like Theophilus (and to rich people like many of us): Here's how you can be rich and absolutely blow it, and here's how you can be rich and be a model of Christian commitment.

Threading the Eye of a Needle

So how can the rich enter the kingdom of heaven? What does it look like for rich Christians to "get it"? Importantly, "getting it" doesn't mean feeling constant shame for being rich. It doesn't have to mean trading places with the poor. And it doesn't mean constant denunciations of income disparity or the assumption that all wealth is exploitative.

But it does mean something. A lot, actually. According to Luke-Acts, to be a rich Christian who "gets it" means (at least) these seven things:

1. We believe. Christ is our everything, our all in all.
   We cannot serve two masters.

2. We repent. We turn from any cheating, swindling, or lying, and we make amends with those we have mistreated.

3. We put Jesus before profit.

4. We are generous. We give freely to help the poor and to further the cause of the gospel.

5. We are good stewards. We don't try to manipulate our way to God by lying, putting on a show, or trying to accrue power with our wealth. We are always shrewd but never power hungry.

6. We do not trust in our money. There is no real security in dollars and cents. The righteous rich do not expect their earthly riches to last. They live for the heavenly riches that do.

7. We demonstrate humility. We consider everything we have to be a gift from God. We are meek before others and meek before God.

In other words, Luke—that great evangelist to the rich—teaches exactly what Paul tells Timothy:

As for the rich in this present age, charge them not to be haughty, nor to set their hopes on the uncertainty of riches, but on God, who richly provides us with everything to enjoy. They are to do good, to be rich in good works, to be generous and ready to share, thus storing up treasure for themselves as a good foundation for the future, so that they may take hold of that which is truly life. (1 Tim. 6:17–19)

Yes, the camel can make it through the eye of the needle. Wealth brings with it many dangers. The love of money is a root of all kinds of evil (1 Tim. 6:10). But, by God's grace, rich Christians—good, faithful Christians—are not as rare as fairies. We must not let our guard down. We must be changed by the gospel. If the materially rich (and that's most of us) are to follow Jesus with integrity, they need a new heart toward God, a new generosity toward people, and a new attitude toward money. With Luke as our guide, we can see that there are many examples of the well-connected and well-to-do getting it right. It is possible to be rich in things without being impoverished toward God.

5

The Infinite Extensibility
of Guilt

IF YOU GREW UP going to school in the United States, almost certainly at some point you had to read *The Scarlet Letter*. Nathaniel Hawthorne's 1850 work about the (supposedly) oppressive legalism of Puritan Massachusetts in the 1640s has become a classic of American literature. The story revolves around Hester Prynne, whose adulterous liaison is obvious to the whole community when she gives birth to her daughter, Pearl. As punishment for her crime, Hester must stand on the scaffold in town, be subject to public ridicule, and wear a scarlet *A* for the rest of her life.

As the story unfolds—spoilers ahead! (but, hey, you've had almost two hundred years to read the book)—we learn that

Hester's thought-to-be-dead husband has settled in Boston and is intent on revenge. Going by the name Roger Chillingworth, he reveals himself to no one but Hester. When Hester and Pearl are shunned by the community, they take refuge outside of Boston and find help from the talented minister, Arthur Dimmesdale, who is himself suffering from some sort of psychological affliction. As you probably remember from your high school lit class, Dimmesdale is, in fact, the guilty lover and Pearl's father. Tormented by his tortured conscience, Dimmesdale eventually mounts the scaffold together with Hester and Pearl and confesses his sins. He immediately dies. A year later, Chillingworth dies. Pearl gets married and moves away. Hester lives alone and resumes her life of good works. When Hester dies, she is buried next to Dimmesdale, and they share a single tombstone marked by a scarlet "A."

I went to high school in the early 1990s, and even back then, in a conservative part of the country, I learned *The Scarlet Letter* as a story about how terrible the judgmental Puritans could be. Whether Hawthorne accurately represented Puritan New England or understood the Christian concepts of repentance, faith, and forgiveness was beside the point. *The Scarlet Letter* was a picture of how miserable life can be when moral standards are absolutely unbending, when sin can never be expunged, and when a community punishes its malefactors with ostracism and humiliation.

Some things never change.

The Guilt We Can't Seem to Shake

While I don't think Hawthorne did right by the Puritans as a whole, he did understand something about human nature, the role of the conscience, and the power of stigma. Although most people reading *The Scarlet Letter* today would prize themselves as being much more enlightened than colonial New England, you only have to visit the land of Twitter for an hour to realize that shunning and shaming are alive and well in our modern world. Sometimes the proverbial scarlet letters are placed around our necks intentionally by those who mean to cast us out of polite society, but other times the mounting shame seems simply natural, an unavoidable part of living in a world marked (we are told) by sexism, racism, ageism, homophobia, and environmental degradation.

A few years ago, in a periodical called *The Hedgehog Review*, there was a fascinating and important article written by Wilfred McClay, then a professor at the University of Oklahoma and now a professor at Hillsdale College. The article was entitled "The Strange Persistence of Guilt." Here's the opening paragraph:

Those of us living in the developed countries of the West find ourselves in the tightening grip of a paradox, one whose shape and character have so far largely eluded our understanding. It is the strange persistence of guilt as a psychological force in modern life. If anything, the word *persistence* understates the matter. Guilt has not merely lingered. It has grown, even metastasized, into an ever more powerful and pervasive element in the life of the contemporary West, even as the rich language formerly used to define it has withered and faded from discourse, and the means of containing its effects, let alone obtaining relief from it, have become ever more elusive.[5]

McClay argues that despite the best efforts of Nietzsche and Freud, guilt has not been eradicated. Nietzsche believed that by the "death" of God, humans would no longer carry around a sense of indebtedness, while Freud tried to "demoralize" guilt by explaining it away as a subjective and emotional pathology. But now well into the twenty-first century, we see

5 Wilfred M. McClay, "The Strange Persistence of Guilt," *The Hedgehog Review* 19 (Spring 2017). Parts of this summary of McClay's article can be found in my chapter "Justification for Today," in *The Reformation and the Irrepressible Word of God: Interpretation, Theology, and Practice*, ed. Scott Manetsch (Downers Grove, IL: IVP Academic, 2019).

that Nietzsche's aggressive secularism and Freud's therapeutic revolution have proven no match for the nagging sense most of us feel that we aren't doing enough and that what we are doing is not good enough.

For the nonreligious, the situation is especially dire, as they have to deal with the residual effects of a Christian conception of sin without the Christian categories of salvation and atonement. And yet, even for the Christian, the psychological toll is real. Part of the problem is what McClay calls the "infinite extensibility of guilt." In our massively connected world—where we can fly anywhere, phone anywhere, get the news from anywhere, and see pictures from anywhere—we cannot help but feel weighed down by suffering on a global scale. With increased capability comes increased culpability. It used to be that we were largely ignorant of the troubles that beset billions of people on the planet. But now when there is a hurricane or an earthquake or a homicide or a traffic accident or a shooting spree or an act of terrorism, we can hear about it instantly. Consequently, we feel like there is always more we can do. We could give another dollar or send another teddy bear or purchase another goat. The circle of obligation feels limitless. Life feels like ten thousand victims on the side of the road, and we are told we must be the good Samaritan in every instance.

The problem is further compounded by the fact that, according to many leading voices inside and outside the church, most of us are complicit in a host of evils that are inherent in the structures and systems of our world. The food you eat? Not ethically sourced. The sports you watch? Exploitation from billionaire owners. The vacation you are looking forward to? The campground was stolen from someone else, and the transportation it takes to get there is overheating the planet. Everywhere we turn, we are told how bad we are and how bad we have been. Forget about the Ten Commandments; there are a million calculations we must make if we are to walk in righteousness and justice.

Part of the System?

We are people loaded with guilt. Sometimes we are conscious of it; more often it's a low-level sense that we are not doing enough, that we have way more than other people on the planet, that the problems in the world could be our fault, and that we really need to do *something*. Zacchaeus is often held up as our example to follow. He didn't just apologize for his sins; he made restitution for the crimes he had committed. And that's right. Restitution makes perfect sense and is eminently biblical, when the person who cheated pays back the person whom they cheated. Zacchaeus generously gave away half of his possessions to the poor in addition to making restitution for those he sinned against. But Zacchaeus did not make restitution with the world or with every poor person in Judea. Instead, he sought to restore fourfold (according to Exodus 22:1) anyone he defrauded (Luke 19:8).

Obedience was straightforward for Zacchaeus in a way it often isn't (but should be) for us. If Zacchaeus felt complicit in the whole system of tax collecting—and surely, the Roman Empire did some bad stuff with those tax dollars—why do we have no record of him leaving the profession? Why did Jesus show kindness to tax collectors (even calling one to be his disciple) without ever commanding them to leave the "system" behind? When the tax collectors came to John the Baptist to be baptized and asked, "What shall we do?" John did not reprimand them for being part of a system designed to plunder the poor. He told them much more simply, "Collect no more than you are authorized to do" (Luke 3:13).

Similarly, neither John the Baptist nor Jesus ever castigated Roman soldiers for being complicit in an imperial system designed to maintain Rome's control over subjugated peoples. Instead, John told them to stop cheating, stop threatening, stop lying, and be content with their wages (Luke 3:14). With tax collectors and soldiers throughout the Gospels, there is no talk of restitution for imperial supremacy or extractive systems, nor any summons to dismantle the structures they inhabited; there is just the straightforward command to live a godly life, be generous to others, and repay what you have stolen.

More to the point, is it a workable ethic, for anyone, to insist that every connection to human sinfulness, past or present, renders us culpable for that sin? Even if we could rid ourselves of every place and every institution tainted by slavery, for example, could we be sure that what remained was never built by people who exploited others and never financed by people who made their money through sinful enterprise? Do not all our favorite streaming services make money, at least in part, by the commodification of sex? Aren't many of our movie studios, and some of our favorite sports leagues, complicit in aiding and abetting a government that disregards basic human rights? Are we sure about the purity of our mutual funds, or of the clothes and shoes that are manufactured overseas, or of the labor practices of the online retailers we use every day? And what of the products we enjoy (or the ones we don't even know we are benefiting from) that may have ties to companies complicit in the past crimes and aggressions of other countries? Christian obedience becomes impossible when, instead of the basics of putting off the works of the flesh and putting on the fruit of the Spirit (Gal.

5:16–24; Col. 3:5–14) we are called to account for every unpopular *ism*, every broken system, and every bad thing we see too much of in the culture.

Corporate Responsibility, but with Limits

This leads to a related question: What about the sins of the past? It's one thing to say that we aren't automatically guilty by virtue of living and working within a fallen system. We live in a globally connected world, and the lines of complicity are hard to trace out. But what about instances where the evils have been obvious and have been committed by people like us? Do we share some responsibility for the sins committed by those who were part of the same immediate family? What about the same religious family? Or what if the perpetrators in the past shared our same skin color? In short, how should we think of corporate responsibility?

Let me state my answer up front and then show how I reach that conclusion: the Bible has a category for corporate responsibility, but there are important limits to the use of this category.

The book of Acts is an illuminating case study in this respect. On the one hand, God may hold people responsible for sins they may not have directly carried out. In Acts 2, Peter charges the "men of Judea and all who dwell in Jerusalem"

(v. 14) with crucifying Jesus (vv. 23, 36). To be sure, they did this by the hands of lawless men (v. 23). But as Jews present in Jerusalem during Passion Week, they bore some responsibility for Jesus's death. Likewise, Peter charged the men of Israel gathered at Solomon's Portico with delivering Jesus over and denying him in the presence of Pilate (Acts 3:11–16). While we don't know if every single person in the Acts 3 crowd had chosen Barabbas over Christ, Peter certainly felt comfortable in laying the crucifixion at their feet. Most, if not all of them, had played an active role in the events leading up to Jesus's death. This was a sin in need of repentance (3:19, 26). We see the same in Acts 4:10 and 5:30 where Peter and John charged the council (i.e., the Sanhedrin) with killing Jesus. In short, the Jews in Jerusalem during Jesus's last days bore responsibility for his murder.

Once the action leaves Jerusalem, however, the charges start to sound different. In speaking to Cornelius (a Gentile), his relatives, and his close friends, Peter relays that they (the Jews in Jerusalem) put Jesus to death (10:39). Even more specifically, Paul tells the crowd in Pisidian Antioch that "those who live in Jerusalem and their rulers" condemned Jesus (Acts 13:27). This speech is especially important because Paul is talking to Jews. He does not blame the Jews in Pisidian Antioch for the crimes of the Jews in Jerusalem.

This is a consistent pattern. Paul doesn't charge the Jews in Thessalonica or Berea with killing Jesus (Acts 17), nor the Jews in Corinth (Acts 18) or in Ephesus (Acts 19). In fact, when Paul returns to Jerusalem years after the crucifixion, he does not accuse the Jews there of killing Jesus; he does not even charge the council with that crime (Acts 23). He doesn't blame Felix (Acts 24) or Festus (Acts 25) or Agrippa (Acts 26) for Jesus's death, even though they are all men in authority connected in some way with the governing apparatus that killed Christ. The apostles considered the Jews in Jerusalem at the time of the crucifixion uniquely responsible for Jesus's death, but this culpability did not extend to every high-ranking official, to every Jew, or to everyone who would live in Jerusalem thereafter. The rest of the Jews and Gentiles in the book of Acts still had to repent of their wickedness, but they were not charged with killing the Messiah.

Does this mean there is never any place for corporate culpability across time and space? No. In Matthew 23:35, Jesus charges the scribes and Pharisees with murdering Zechariah the son of Barachiah. Although there is disagreement about who this Zechariah is, most scholars agree he is a figure from the past who was not killed in their lifetimes. The fact that the scribes and Pharisees were treating Jesus with contempt put them in the same category as their ancestors who had also treated God's prophets with contempt (cf. Acts 7:51–53). It could rightly be said that they murdered Zechariah between the sanctuary and the altar because they shared in the same spirit of hate as the murderers in Zechariah's day.

Similarly, there are several examples of corporate confession in the Old Testament. As God's covenant people, the Israelites were commanded to confess their sins and turn from their wicked ways so as to come out from under the divinely sanctioned covenant curses (2 Chron. 6:12–42; 7:13–18). This is why we see the likes of Ezra (Ezra 9–10), Nehemiah (Neh. 1:4–11), and Daniel (Dan. 9:3–19) leading in corporate confession. The Jews were not lumped together because of race, ethnicity, geography, education level, or socioeconomic status. The Israelites had freely entered into a covenant relationship with each other and with their God. In all three examples above, the leader entered into corporate confession because (1) he was praying for the covenant people, (2) the people were as a whole marked by unfaithfulness, and (3) the leader himself bore some responsibility for the actions of the people, either by having been blind to the sin (Ezra 9:3) or by participating directly in the sin (Neh. 1:6; Dan. 9:20). Culpability for sins committed can extend to a large group *if virtually everyone in the group was active in the sin or if we bear the same spiritual resemblance to the perpetrators of the past.*

It also bears mentioning that public apologies are more or less appropriate based on whether their cost is mainly to us or mainly to someone else. When someone steeped in Southern Presbyterianism apologizes in tears for the sins of the nineteenth-century Presbyterians he grew up revering, that costs something. When college kids who have never been tempted in their lives to idolize Richard the Lionheart set up confessional booths on campus to apologize for the Crusades, that costs next to nothing. One is a public expression of personal lament; the other is a personal expression of public virtue (of our own) and public accusation (of others).

Sour Grapes

Jeremiah 31:29–30 is an important text:

In those days they shall no longer say:

> "The fathers have eaten sour grapes,
> and the children's teeth are set on edge."

But everyone shall die for his own iniquity. Each man who eats sour grapes, his teeth shall be set on edge.

The proverb about eating sour grapes is also quoted in Ezekiel 18:2 and suggests that the people of Judah believed God was being unjust in punishing them for the sins of past generations (18:25). "Why should the children be punished for the sins of their fathers?" they asked. But Jeremiah and Ezekiel quote the proverb to reject it. The soul who sins shall die, not the soul of the one who does not sin (Ezek. 18:4–9).

Although Jeremiah and Ezekiel speak of the proverb being no more used in Israel, the reality of the proverb was never the way God dealt with his people. It is true that God had promised to visit "the iniquity of the fathers on the children to the third and the fourth generation of those who hate me" and to show "steadfast love to thousands of those who love me and keep my commandments" (Exod. 20:5–6). But do not miss the precise language of God's promise. God says he will visit the iniquity of *those who hate me* and will show steadfast love to those who love me and keep my commandments. The promise was based on the children behaving like their parents, not simply on account of parental behavior irrespective of whether the children deviated from that pattern.

Long before Jeremiah and Ezekiel, it was already a principle in the Mosaic covenant that the corporate nature of the covenant did not consign children to the punishment of their fathers. "Fathers shall not be put to death because of their children, nor shall children be put to death because of their fathers. Each one shall be put to death for his own sin" (Deut. 24:16). It was never the case that children, regardless of how they lived, were to be punished for their father's sins.

Living life in the present is hard enough without the impossible burden of owning the sins of the past as well. To be sure, our parents can give us huge advantages or disadvantages in life, and on a cosmic scale (known only to God) some of us enter this world with more privileges than others. We should also add that past sins can be *recognized* and *renounced*, even if we are not required specifically to *repent* of them. The sins of the past are far from irrelevant. And yet we are not meant to live with a sense of corporate guilt for an ethnic, racial, or biological identity we did not choose and from which we cannot be free. Self-flagellation is not a requirement for spiritual maturity. It is one thing for us to love God and love our neighbors; it is quite another if the call of Christian discipleship means we must, on account of the failures of others, hate ourselves.

6

Sermon (of Misery?) on the Mount

THE SERMON ON THE MOUNT is undoubtedly the most famous sermon ever preached. Jesus's teaching in Matthew 5–7 has some of the most familiar phrases and lines and sections in the whole Bible: blessed are the poor in spirit, salt and light, go the extra mile, love your enemies, the Lord's Prayer, treasures in heaven, seek first the kingdom, judge not, the Golden Rule, the narrow gate, build your house on the rock, and on and on. Even many non-Christians have heard of the Sermon on the Mount, or at least they know the familiar phrases (even if they don't know where they came from). If we want to know what it looks like to follow Jesus, surely these three chapters in Matthew give us as clear a picture as any other section in the Gospels.

As famous as this sermon is, you would think there would be more agreement about what it says. One scholar I read cited a recent survey with thirty-six different interpretations. Another commentator mentioned eight wrong approaches before he got to the right approach. Even when Christians agree on what Jesus teaches in the Sermon on the Mount, they disagree on how (or whether) we are meant to apply Jesus's instructions. In particular, Christians often approach these three chapters like they are stepping into the ring for a game of *Mike Tyson's Punch-Out!!* We read each successive verse as if Jesus meant to trap us in a corner, pummel us into submission, and knock us to the ground. Don't be angry in your heart—smack! Don't look at someone lustfully—bam! Don't store up treasures on earth—kapow! The Sermon on the Mount, it seems, is designed to convince every follower of Jesus that they are terrible followers of Jesus.

Making Sense of the Mountain Message

But is that really the best way to understand the Sermon on the Mount? Was the overarching point of Jesus's teaching to convince his disciples that he was calling them to a life of unremitting failure? Let's step back and try to understand the Sermon on the Mount in its context and on its own terms.

First, we should note that the Sermon on the Mount is part of a larger pattern in Matthew's Gospel. The Sermon on the Mount is special because it is such a large chunk of uninterrupted teaching from Jesus. It's also special because of the attention Christians have given it throughout the years. But in another sense, it's one of many distinct teaching sections in Matthew's Gospel. After an opening prologue about Jesus's origin and birth (Matt. 1:1–2:23), Matthew organizes his material into five sections, each having the same pattern: a narrative about the kingdom, then a discourse about the kingdom, then a transition statement into the next section.

- Section 1: The introduction of the kingdom (narrative 2:1–4:25; discourse 5:1–7:29; transition 7:28–29)

- Section 2: The in-breaking of the kingdom (narrative 8:1–10:4; discourse 10:5–11:1; transition 11:1)

- Section 3: Opposition to the kingdom (narrative 11:2–12:50; discourse 13:1–53; transition 13:53)

- Section 4: Division on account of the kingdom (narrative 13:54–17:27; discourse 18:1–19:2; transition 19:1–2)

- Section 5: Seeming defeat and the ultimate triumph of the kingdom (narrative 19:3–23:39; discourse 24:1–25:46; transition 26:1–5)

After these five sections, we have a conclusion focusing on Jesus's death and resurrection to mirror the prologue, which focused on Jesus's origin and birth. The book ends with a summons to take the commands of Jesus and go make disciples of all nations.

Interesting, you say, but what does this have to do with how we interpret the Sermon on the Mount? Well, if the Sermon on the Mount is part of the larger structure and progression in Matthew's Gospel, then we can't make the sermon about something other than what the rest of the book is about. Matthew is clearly not about a legalistic summons to earn your way into heaven. After all, we read from the beginning that Jesus came to save his people from their sins (Matt. 1:21). But neither is Matthew about Jesus's plan to teach about a kingdom no one can enter, lay out a course of discipleship that no one can pass, and make commands that no one can really follow. When the book ends with Jesus telling the eleven disciples to teach all that he has commanded, there is no asterisk that says, "Ha, ha, but obviously no one can really obey any of my commandments."

This leads to the second principle we must keep in mind as we approach and apply the Sermon on the Mount: the sermon is about the kingdom. We see this in the opening and closing of these chapters (Matt. 5:3; 7:21–23) and all throughout the sermon (5:10, 17–20; 6:10, 33). The Sermon on the Mount is the explication of what it means to repent and receive the gospel of the kingdom (4:17, 23). Jesus's message is not about building the kingdom, creating the kingdom, or expanding the kingdom. It's about his people living like God's reign and rule have come into their lives.

Third, the Sermon on the Mount is also about discipleship. While the crowds had once again gathered to hear Jesus by the end of Matthew 7, the sermon explicitly began as an opportunity to teach Jesus's disciples (5:1). We import later theological content into the term *disciple* and assume that these are regenerate, justified believers. By *disciple*, at this point in Jesus's ministry, he simply means those who are following Jesus from place to place and are eager to hear what he has to say. The Sermon on the Mount answers the question, "What does this kingdom stuff involve? What is it like to be a follower of Jesus?"

Fourth, the Sermon on the Mount is a reapplication of God's law. The first several chapters of Matthew draw a number of parallels between Jesus and Moses. There is the death threat by a jealous king, the coming out of Egypt, the crossing of the

Jordan River (like the Red Sea), the wilderness temptations for forty days (like Israel endured for forty years), and the going up on a mountain to receive instructions from God's lawgiver. Jesus is the new Moses deepening the force of the Ten Commandments and explaining what it looks like to live as a kingdom of priests. To be sure, the Sermon on the Mount, like the Ten Commandments, reveals our need for a Savior, but it does more than that. It also shows us how we should live as God's people.

An Impossible Standard?

If we approach the Sermon on the Mount only or mainly as a means by which we see our sinfulness, we've not taken the sermon on its own terms. Martyn Lloyd-Jones saw the situation clearly:

Is it not true to say of many of us that in actual practice our view of the doctrine of grace is such that we scarcely ever take the plain teaching of the Lord Jesus Christ seriously? We have so emphasized the teaching that all is of grace and that we ought not to try to imitate His example in order to make ourselves Christians, that we are virtually in the position of ignoring His teaching altogether and of saying that it has nothing to do with us because we are under grace. Now I wonder how seriously we take the gospel of our Lord and Savior Jesus Christ. The best way of concentrating on the question is, I think, to face the Sermon on the Mount.[6]

Lloyd-Jones is exactly right. We've turned the Sermon on the Mount into a giant spanking spoon—good for making you squeal in pain, but not a welcome instrument or a way of life. The Great Commission, then, becomes a summons to teach the nations everything Jesus has said—which, of course, they cannot do, and he doesn't expect them to observe.

But isn't the Sermon on the Mount an impossible standard? Who among us never worries, never lusts, never gets angry, never lies, is never a hypocrite, and always loves his enemies, always follows the Golden Rule, and always serves God alone? Here it's good to recall the distinction between true obedience and perfect obedience. There is a way to insist on genuine obedience as a way of life without doubling down on *never* sinning and *always* doing what is right. Besides that helpful theological category, however, notice four things in the text pointing us away from thinking Jesus means to give us an impossible discipleship plan.

First, Jesus presents us with bracing either/or options at several points in his sermon. We can take the narrow gate or the wide gate, the easy path or the hard path, the way of life or the way

6 D. Martyn Lloyd-Jones, *Studies in the Sermon on the Mount* (Grand Rapids, MI: Eerdmans, 1976), 1:12–13.

of death (Matt. 7:13–14). We can be healthy trees bearing good fruit or diseased trees bearing bad fruit (7:17–20). We can build our house on the rock and be secure or build our house on the sand and be destroyed (7:24–27). The stakes could not be higher. If we are no more righteous than the scribes and Pharisees, we will never enter the kingdom of heaven (5:20). If we murder in our hearts, we are liable to the hell of fire (5:22). If we give ourselves over to lust, we will end up in hell (5:29). If we don't do the will of our Father, we will not enter the kingdom of heaven (7:21). We must not give up hope of obeying Jesus's commands, lest we give up the hope of heaven.

Too many Christians instinctively set aside the commands of Scripture as utterly impossible to obey on any level. The danger with this mindset is not only that we might be disheartened when we shouldn't be, but that we might not be warned when we *should* be. Once we convince ourselves that failure is the norm—"No one really obeys Jesus. No one really builds his house on the rock. No one really is pure of heart. No one really enters the narrow gate. No one really bears good fruit."—we won't take seriously the many warnings given to us in Scripture that people unchanged by the gospel prove themselves to never really have been saved by the gospel (1 Cor. 6:9–10; Heb. 12:14; Rev. 21:8). When genuine (though imperfect) discipleship becomes impossible, hell often becomes impossible as well. By contrast, Jesus in the Sermon on the Mount urges us to choose the right way to live and stick with it.

Second, Jesus understands that there is an already-and-not-yet dimension to our Christian walk. On the one hand, Jesus announces that the kingdom of heaven is at hand (Matt. 4:17). On the other hand, he also tells us to pray for the kingdom to come (6:10). The fact that we have to pray for God's will to be done on earth as it is in heaven implies that we are not always angelic in our obedience. Heaven has broken in but is not yet fully and finally come to earth (Rev. 11:15).

Third, woven into the fabric of Christ's kingdom living is the expectation that we will need grace and forgiveness. This is a key observation, and one we often miss. When Jesus exhorts us to "[hear] these words of mine and [do] them" (Matt. 7:24), he's thinking of all the words he's just been preaching. And think about what we find among those words. "Blessed are the poor in spirit" (5:3). "Blessed are those who mourn" (5:4). "Forgive us our debts" (6:12). And in Luke's account: "Be merciful, even as your Father is merciful" (Luke 6:36). The Sermon on the Mount contains within its many commands an awareness that these commands will not be kept flawlessly. That means part of entering by the narrow gate is being so poor in spirit that you know you need God's help. It means lamenting your sins and looking to God for mercy. It means asking your heavenly

Father to forgive the debts you accrue daily. Jesus's sermon is not a mount of self-defeating misery, because part of observing all that Jesus commanded is knowing where to find relief when we are miserable offenders.

This may be a good spot to say something about the importance of the conscience. The normal state of the Christian should not be one of low- to medium-level guilt. Remember, Paul said the conscience accuses *and* excuses us (Rom. 2:15). The conscience is supposed to be a prosecuting attorney when we sin and a defense attorney when we don't sin. And yet many Christians operate with the assumption that if they are truly spiritual, they will feel bad all the time. That wasn't Paul's approach. He boasted in the testimony of his conscience (2 Cor. 1:12) and even went so far as to say he wasn't aware of anything against himself (1 Cor. 4:4). That didn't mean he was sinless. In fact, he quickly acknowledged that the Lord was the ultimate judge and he might be judging himself incorrectly. But his goal as a Christian was to serve the Lord with a clean conscience, and he frequently boasted of doing so in his ministry (Acts 23:1; Rom. 9:1; 1 Tim. 1:5; 2 Tim. 1:3).

In other words, when Paul sinned, he felt convicted, which prompted him to repent, which allowed him to know the grace of God and have a clean conscience. And when he didn't sin, he didn't manufacture a guilty conscience. He wasn't going to make himself feel bad in order to make his opponents happy. If we are to follow Paul's example, we too should always take pains to have a clear conscience toward both God and man (Acts 24:16). Don't train yourself to have a guilty conscience. If you are guilty, deal with it and know the joy of forgiveness in Christ. If you aren't guilty, don't wallow in feelings of failure as if that makes you a better Christian.

Fourth, the Sermon on the Mount is not an impossible standard, because pleasing Jesus is not impossible. With most sermons, the messenger should decrease so that message can increase. But when you are the Messiah, the Son of the living God, the point of the preaching is going to be the preacher himself. The Sermon on the Mount compels us to ask: Who is this that thinks we will be persecuted for *his* sake (Matt. 5:11), that religious tradition bows before *him* (5:21–22, 27–28, 31–32, 33–34, 38–39, 43–44), that building a life on *his* words makes one wise (7:24), that the final judgment will be given with reference to *him* and given by *him* (7:23)? Of course, the first and lasting impression of the sermon was Jesus's authority (7:28–29). No one had preached like Jesus before because there never was a God-man like Jesus before.

Walking in the way of the Sermon on the Mount means walking close to Jesus. The relentless subplot to this entire sermon comes in the form of this question: Are you with me?

Are you *really* with me? Are you with me no matter what? Submitting to this sermon means finally and fully submitting to Jesus. The law in the Sermon on the Mount reflects the heart of the lawgiver. The commands of Jesus are not meant to crush us any more than Jesus means to crush us. Jesus came to save us (Matt. 1:21), to enlist us (16:24), and to be with us until the end of the age (28:20). To the unbelieving and unrepentant Jesus will be a terror (11:20–24), but to all who know the Son, to those who look for rest in the Son, to those who are eager to walk with the Son and learn from the Son, the yoke he gives you is easy, and the burden he asks you to carry is light (11:30).

7

Please and Thank You

I IMAGINE MOST authors have had the same experience. After you write a book, you tend to get requests to speak on the same topic. Since *The Hole in Our Holiness* came out in 2012, I've preached and taught on sanctification many times, often using material from one of the chapters of the book. Without a doubt, I've gotten the strongest response whenever I've taught from chapter 5, "The Pleasure of God and the Possibility of Godliness."[7] I'm not exaggerating when I say that people sometimes came up to me in tears, saying, "How did I miss this my whole Christian life?" It wasn't my teaching that was impressive. It was the truth itself that impressed people. "Wait, God can really be pleased with me? I don't have to settle for being a justified, heaven-bound

7   Kevin DeYoung, *The Hole in Our Holiness: Filling the Gap between Gospel Passion and the Pursuit of Godliness* (Wheaton, IL: Crossway, 2012), 63–77.

failure? I can live an obedient life and know the smile of God?" In some ways, what you have been reading is the book-length harvest that grew from those fifteen pages of sowing seed.

The point is worth making again: Christians are not only counted righteous on account of Christ's righteousness (2 Cor. 5:21); we can—as the fruit, not the ground, of that imputed righteousness—live holy lives pleasing to God. Just look at some of the verses that speak of God's pleasure in our obedience:

> I know, my God, that you test the heart and have pleasure in uprightness. (1 Chron. 29:17)

> His delight is not in the strength of the horse,
>   nor his pleasure in the legs of a man,
> but the LORD takes pleasure in those who fear him,
>   in those who hope in his steadfast love. (Ps. 147:10–11)

> I am well supplied, having received from Epaphroditus the gifts you sent, a fragrant offering, a sacrifice acceptable and pleasing to God. (Phil. 4:18)

> [May you] walk in a manner worthy of the Lord, fully pleasing to him: bearing fruit in every good work and increasing in the knowledge of God. (Col. 1:10)

Children, obey your parents in everything, for this pleases the Lord. (Col. 3:20)

First of all, then, I urge that supplications, prayers, intercessions, and thanksgivings be made for all people. . . . This is good, and it is pleasing in the sight of God our Savior. (1 Tim. 2:1, 3)

If a widow has children or grandchildren, let them first learn to show godliness to their own household and to make some return to their parents, for this is pleasing in the sight of God. (1 Tim. 5:4)

Do not neglect to do good and to share what you have, for such sacrifices are pleasing to God. (Heb. 13:16)

Whatever we ask we receive from him, because we keep his commandments and do what pleases him. (1 John 3:22)

This is not the picture of a peevish and austere God. Rather, we can deduce from these verses that whenever we walk in uprightness, whenever we share with others, whenever we fear the Lord, in short, whenever we obey the commandments from a sincere heart, God is pleased.

We have a tendency to so focus on God as Judge that we forget to relate to him as Father. Both ideas are important; one must not be used to flatten the other. The doctrine of justification is about God as our judge. We are guilty or innocent, condemned or declared righteous, on our way to heaven or on our way to hell. The relationship is binary: we are in, or we are out. Those are biblical categories. But our relationship with God does not just exist in a courtroom; it exists in a family room. It is significant, is it not, that when Jesus taught the disciples to pray, he instructed them to approach God as their father. And that means a dynamic relationship instead of a binary one. As a father, God can be angry with his children, and he sometimes must discipline the children he loves. But as a father, God can (and does!) take delight in his children.

I have a gaggle of children, so I am always issuing forth commands (sometimes in a spirit of grace and love, and sometimes not so much). Because my kids are kids, they don't always obey promptly and cheerfully. Okay, sometimes they don't obey at all. But at other times, they listen, they move, they smile, and they obey. Not perfectly, but truly. If I tell my older boys to clean their room—a command less likely to be obeyed than if it were given to my oldest daughter (actually, her room would already be clean)—and they march right upstairs, and with their hearts strangely warmed they work together and put their mess in order, how would I respond? I wouldn't shame them for getting some things in the wrong place or for not being up to the level of their mom (or, reaching to the seventh heaven, the level of my mother-in-law). I wouldn't roll my eyes because the socks were folded somewhat poorly and the bed sheets were tussled. No, if they worked hard, worked gladly, and worked without delay, I would, after lifting myself off the ground, be extremely pleased. Dads delight in their children whenever they trust and obey.

The pleasure of our heavenly Father is one of the main motivations for the Christian life. We make it our aim to please God (2 Cor. 5:9). We know the Lord takes pleasure in his people (Ps. 149:4) and is pleased with a broken and contrite heart (Ps. 51:16–17). Therefore, we are urged as believers to please God (1 Thess. 4:1) and to discern what is pleasing to the Lord (Eph. 5:10). If we think God is impossible to please, we must think he is incapable of doing anything praiseworthy with and through his children. We need not live our lives with eyes to the ground, hoping the divine taskmaster looks the other way. On the contrary, we know it is possible to please our heavenly Father because he works in us what is pleasing in his sight (Heb. 13:21).

Character before Time Commitments

"And what do you suggest I *stop* doing?"

That's what I often think when others besides God love me and have a wonderful plan for my life. Sometimes the suggestions come from well-meaning friends. Sometimes the suggestions are more like demands, and they come from Internet "friends" who think I should be more attentive to their passions and concerns. I'm sure you've had the same experience. You are already maxed out with responsibilities at work and at home. You are already barely getting enough sleep and hardly finding any time for rest or leisure. You are already squeezed past the margins of your life, and then someone wants you to do more. Okay, but if I am going to be involved in this new good thing, I'll need help knowing what current good things I should not keep doing.

I don't recall when it dawned on me, but the realization has been a major breakthrough: the Bible emphasizes character, not time commitments. When I'm told to put to death the deeds of the flesh, or to make a covenant with my eyes, or to refrain from lying, or to not covet, or to not take the Lord's name in vain, or to be generous, or to be humble instead of haughty, they are hard commands. I won't grow in this sort of godliness quickly or easily. It's important to note that these commands don't require me to be well-researched in the causes of poverty, or to spearhead a clean water initiative, or to master the art of time management in order to be obedient.

No doubt, God's word does make demands on our time. Honoring aging parents will take time. Showing hospitality will take time. I may have to look into long-term care facilities or figure out how to make the new international family feel welcome. Love is willing to bear burdens for others. But these tasks are not impossible, and what they require is personal and neighborly rather than programmatic and societal. The scope is limited and specific. God may ask me to change my priorities. He does not ask me to change the world.

The virtue lists of the New Testament are instructive in this regard. When the Bible wants to tell us what Christians are like, it gives us character traits, not a to-do list. Christians are full of love, joy, peace, patience, kindness, goodness, faithfulness, gentleness, and self-control (Gal. 5:22–23). Christians are marked by compassionate hearts, humility, meekness, bearing with one another, and forgiving one another (Col. 3:12–15). Christians are not envious, not boastful, not arrogant, not rude, not selfish, not irritable, and not resentful; they take no joy in wrongdoing, and they rejoice in the truth (1 Cor. 13:4–7). Christians make every effort to add to their faith virtue, knowledge, self-control, steadfastness, godliness, brotherly affection, and love (2 Pet. 1:5–7). Expressing the right feelings and signing up for the right causes are less important than growing in this Christlike character. "Take Time to Be Holy" makes for a better hymn than "Take Time to Be a Revolutionary."

One of the reasons Christianity can feel impossible is that we've concocted a Christianity unsuitable for finite creatures. If I had an infinite supply of time, money, and energy, I wouldn't have to make any hard choices. I could keep on adding without ever subtracting. But, of course, we are not infinite beings. We have limits—lots of limits, God-given limits, and probably more limits than we realize. I often repeat the insight I first learned from the business guru Peter Drucker; namely, that we don't really have priorities (things at the head of the list we want to do) if we don't have any posteriorities (things at the bottom of the list we won't do). Because the total amount of time in each day is inelastic— we cannot create more of it, and we cannot save more for another day—we have to make hard choices. We simply cannot do everything.

Let me state that last sentence even more provocatively: we cannot even *care* about everything. That may sound heartless, but it's true. You may fancy yourself a big-hearted person who feels deeply for the needs and hurts of others. Good for you.

But even the most compassionate person cannot feel what everyone feels, let alone know but a tiny fraction of all that good people care about in the world. The Internet gives us the illusion of omniscience, and because of that illusion it can feel like we must be omni-empathetic and omnibenevolent. The digital world screams (often literally) for our emotional attention and demands, at all times, that we must say *something!* and do *something!*[8]

The problems with these kinds of demands are manifold.

1. These demands exist because the Internet exists. Go way back in ancient history, to, like, 1999, before the Internet and iPhones were everywhere, when no one expected you to know everything going on in the world and no one expected you to comment on the latest instance of tragedy or stupidity. The definition of true virtue has not been rewritten because you have a smartphone in your pocket.

2. The demands for *something!* push us to certain kinds of proposals. We are pushed toward easy-to-spot "solutions" like electoral politics, government programs, new

---

8 The careful reader may note with irony that I wrote a book called *Just Do Something*. That book was about not getting lost in a sea of subjectivism, while I'm using "do something!" in the context of this book to refer to the demands placed upon us to solve the world's problems. (Kevin DeYoung, *Just Do Something: A Liberating Approach to Finding God's Will* [Chicago: Moody, 2009]).

bureaucracies, and raising awareness. These may or may not contribute to the solution, but they count on the culture's scorecard of virtue, so they are the ones that get all the attention. By contrast, almost no one thinks that a quiet life of building a home, getting involved in church, and cultivating Christlikeness are worthwhile answers to our most vexing problems.

3. The problems about which we must do *something!* are usually the most intractable and complicated problems. No respectable person is for racism, drug addiction, mass shootings, and homelessness. If there were simple ways to solve these problems, they would have been done by now. But the wayward human heart is not so easily tamed. It's one thing for Christians to be told that they must repent of a specific sin (like racism or abortion), or even to be told that there is a particular unjust statute to be overturned (like Jim Crow laws or *Roe v. Wade*). It's another thing to be told that we must repair the very fabric of society so as to eradicate sin or make it unthinkable. While specific Christians will be called to lead the way in specific areas of political or societal concern, it is unreasonable to demand that every Christian needs to say something or do something about everything. There must be a way for followers of Jesus to hear, "Well done, good and faithful servant,"

apart from being political operatives, full-time bloggers, or community organizers.

The demands placed upon us in a world of decreasing distance and increasing guilt are too heavy for mere mortals to bear. The good Samaritan had a duty to care for the beaten man on the side of the road. He did not, however, have a duty to care for all beaten men on the other side of the world. When we insist that we are obliged to be burdened for every person everywhere, we end up making a virtue out of feeling pity, and we end up making our lives grimly pitiful. C. S. Lewis made this point beautifully in a 1946 letter:

> It is one of the evils of rapid diffusion of news that the sorrows of all the world come to us every morning. I think each village was meant to feel pity for *its own* sick and poor whom it can help and I doubt if it is the duty of any private person to fix his mind on ills which he cannot help. (This may even become an *escape* from the works of charity we really *can* do to those we know.) A great many people (not you) do now seem to think that the mere state of being *worried* is in itself meritorious. I don't think it is. We must, if it so happens, give our lives for others; but even while we're doing it, I think we're meant to enjoy Our Lord and,

in Him, our friends, our food, our sleep, our jokes, and the birds song and the frosty sunrise.[9]

If Lewis's words were wise in the middle of the twentieth century, they are even more necessary today. We've equated feeling bad with doing good. Of course, there is the danger that if we don't insist on an obligation to help everyone, we won't bother to help anyone, but every true principle can be abused. And the true principle here is that there is no virtue in the embrace of globalized worry, nor in the repudiation of all earthly joy.

All These Commended through Their Faith

You've probably seen some of the (in)famous mean obituaries before, obituaries so nasty you don't know if you should laugh or cry. For example, the obituary for Kathleen Dehmlow of Wabasso, Minnesota, mentions that she became pregnant by her husband's brother, moved to California, and abandoned her children, Gina and Jay, to be raised by their grandparents. The concluding paragraph observes that Kathleen passed away on May 31 "and will now face judgement." The final line

---

9   C. S. Lewis, *Books, Broadcasts and the War 1931–1949*, vol. 2, *The Collected Letters of C. S. Lewis*, ed. Walter Hooper (San Francisco: HarperOne, 2004), 747–48.

makes doubly sure no one misses the point: "She will not be missed by Gina and Jay, and they understand that this world is a better place without her."[10]

Thankfully, most people's lives can be summed up with a tad more optimism. As a pastor, I've been to my share of funerals, and on every occasion friends and family members have managed to find many good things to celebrate about the deceased. Sometimes *too* many good things. Most people were not as amazing as the funeral eulogy makes them out to be, and most people are not nearly as bad as Ms. Dehmlow was in the eyes of her children.

My aim in this book is not to make bad people seem better than they are, nor is my aim to make impressive people seem flawless. My aim is that we see good and faithful servants of Christ as, well, good and faithful servants of Christ. Hebrews 11:39 says "all these"—Abel, Enoch, Noah, Abraham, Sarah, Isaac, Jacob, Joseph, Moses, Rahab, Gideon, Barak, Samson, Jephthah, David, Samuel, the prophets, and many other unnamed men and women—were "commended through their faith." Two things are noteworthy about that statement. One, that these men and women were commended according to

---

10 "Mean Obituary for Minnesota 80-Year-Old Says She Will Not Be Missed," ABC News, June 5, 2018, https://abc7ny.com/.

what they did through faith. Two, that these men and women were commended at all. This is a motley crew of heroes. We have liars, cheats, doubters, braggarts, prostitutes, murderers, and adulterers. Almost every member of the Hall of Faith could easily be canceled for their sins and mistakes. And yet Scripture presents each one as commendable, not because their sins should be glossed over, but because, by faith in the promises of God, they did mighty deeds. We'll have to wait until we get to heaven to find just how "well done" each one did, but on the whole the writer of Hebrews wants us to see that they got some pretty big things right.

Deep down, I don't think we really believe in this impossible version of Christianity. We know too many people— living and dead—who are worthy examples of Christian discipleship. We've convinced ourselves that true piety means the acceptance of spiritual failure, but we can all think of parents or pastors, or friends or family members, or missionaries or grandmothers who lived like good and faithful servants. They were champions for Christ, not punching bags for God's disappointment.

We think of the apostle Paul as intimidating and stern, but I love to reflect on what a great encourager he was. Paul was always noticing—and then naming—the evidence of grace he saw in others. Tychicus was a faithful minister in the Lord (Eph. 6:21), Epaphroditus a fellow worker and fellow soldier (Phil. 2:25), Onesimus a faithful and beloved brother (Col. 4:9). Luke was a beloved physician (Col. 4:14), Timothy a true child in a common faith (Titus 1:4), and Philemon a beloved fellow worker (Philem. 1). In Romans 16, Paul praised Prisca and Aquila for risking their necks for his life. He sent greetings to the beloved Epaenetus, the beloved Ampliatus, the beloved Stachys, and the beloved Persis. And my favorite: he thanked Rufus's mom for being a mother to him. Paul was deeply affectionate and consistently encouraging. In fact, Paul frequently described the aim of his ministry as boasting in his spiritual children on the last day, implying that there is something in ordinary Christian discipleship that is worth boasting about (Rom. 15:15–18; 2 Cor. 1:12–14; Phil. 2:16–18; 1 Thess. 2:19–20). He knew that faithfulness and courage were possible, and he loved to commend it wherever he saw it.

If Paul can do it, I bet God can too.

8

A Quiet Life

I REMEMBER DISTINCTLY taking a prayer walk as a college student and feeling deeply in my bones, "I want to be a part of changing the world." That wasn't a bad feeling. I really wanted to make a difference for Christ. I was eager to preach the gospel, eager to shake the world out of sin and lethargy, eager to see revival and reformation. I am still eager for those things. God has done amazing things in history with young people who are just crazy enough to try for big things and just idealistic enough to think they might work. This book is not about making "radical" and "passion" bad words.

But they are not the only words, and they aren't always helpful words. While a few people may have personalities that are relentlessly intense about everything, most of us mortals will settle into a life of predictable routines. That word *settle* can be bad if it means passivity, but it can also be a good word if the opposite is constantly being unsettled. Even if you leave everything behind, become a missionary, and live among an unreached people, your life, on most days, will be predictable. After a while, it will likely feel quite ordinary. No matter where we live as Christians, life will be filled with a lot of the same things: eating, sleeping, cleaning, laughing, crying, taking care of kids, going to church (or gathering with other believers as we try to plant a church), praying, reading our Bibles, trying to get along with others, and seeking to make a difference in others' lives. If God isn't happy with "normal" life, he's not going to be happy with most of us, because normal is what most of our days are like.

There is something powerful about the zeal and idealism of younger Christians. If that's you, don't let other believers rain on your parade. But realize that there is something wise about the plodding consistency and steady strength of older Christians. There's no doubt that I'm less "radical" than I was when I was younger. I need to be careful that this doesn't mean I'm less militant against my sin and less open to taking risks for the cause of Christ. I hope what it means is that I'm less prone to wild swings of mood and intention, less prone to morbid introspection, and less prone to judge others who aren't as intense.

Family life has taught me a lot. Marrying a wife who is sanguine in personality and wonderfully phlegmatic (she might prefer the word *relaxed*) about most things has helped me see that there are many different ways to be a mature and loving Christian. Few people are as sweet and caring as my wife. She has been loved and admired in every church we've been a part of, and she would score very low on the intensity scale. Likewise, having many children has shown me that we really do come out of the womb with much of our personality hardwired. Being a parent has also forced me to get used to the mundane, because that's what life is like with children who need baths, and food, and help with their homework, and rides to swim practice, and new shoes, new clothes, new attitudes, and more food.

This is ordinary life, and it is also extraordinary at the same time. One of the great disservices we have done the church is to let people think that getting married, having children, staying married, taking those children to church, teaching those children about the faith, buying shoes, and training those children to be kind and courageous Christian adults is something other than radical discipleship. If we too are "exiles" (1 Pet. 1:1), then Jeremiah's counsel to the Jews in Babylon is good advice for us as well: settle down, raise a family, and seek the welfare of your temporary home (Jer.

29:4–7). When we follow Jesus by loving others, discipling our children (whether biological or spiritual), getting involved in a good church, and sharing with others our faith and our resources—when we do all that, we are most definitely *doing something*.

The Quiet Place

When you are a kid, quiet is the last thing you want. Teachers are always putting a finger to their lips and telling their students to quiet down. Parents are always telling their kids to do something quiet. When you are in church or on a plane or in the movie theater, you need to be quiet. I remember being sent to my room for an hour on Sundays to have a "quiet rest time." Now as a parent, I try (usually in vain) to get my kids to do the same. Judging by their response to "quiet rest time," you'd think I was throwing them into The Hole at Shawshank for a month.

As an adult, the prospect of quiet hits you differently. Granted, empty nesters might tell you that the house can be *too* quiet, but especially in the busy childrearing years, quiet is a rare and precious gift. In the midst of life's everyday chaos, quiet means a chance to read, a chance to think, a chance to sit outside and listen to the sounds of the street or the sounds of nature. "Be still, and know that I am God" (Ps. 46:10) isn't exactly about quietness, but it is about God fighting for us so we can rest. And that's what we need if Christianity is to be a refuge and not a recipe for exhaustion.

Have you ever noticed what Paul tells Timothy to pray for?

First of all, then, I urge that supplications, prayers, inter-cessions, and thanksgivings be made for all people, for kings and all who are in high positions, that we may lead a peaceful and quiet life, godly and dignified in every way. (1 Tim. 2:1–2)

The "that we" is key. We are to pray for all kinds of people, including those in positions of authority and influence, *to the end* that we may lead ordinary lives of faithfulness and integrity. People in high positions have the ability to make life hard for Christians. They can aggressively persecute the church or at least make devotion to Jesus extra difficult and dangerous. Paul doesn't wish for opposition and mistreatment. He'd rather have kings allow Christians to go about their business free from interference and harassment. His prayer is for peace and quiet.

We almost never hear this emphasized in the church. The emphasis is on all that we have to do and all that depends on us. If you told people you were praying for the opportunity to "lead a peaceful and quiet life, godly and dignified in every way," they would more likely accuse you of being a sellout than doing what the Bible urges us to do. You would be accused of reinforcing the status quo, but, of course, "steady on" is only a bad idea if you are heading in the wrong direction. Yes, we absolutely must be salt and light, but why do we think that a life of godliness is not flavorful or that being dignified in every way does not shine bright?

There is something in the expectation of your run-of-the-mill evangelical church (at least in America) that pushes Christians to be energetic and entrepreneurial. There is nothing wrong with those traits, but they are not the only traits we need, and they are not, by themselves, biblical virtues. If we don't want "quiet" to become quietism, neither do we want "active" to become a demand for hyperactivity. At its best, the spirit of evangelicalism reminds the church that nominalism is deadly and that we all need Jesus as Savior and Lord. At its worst, that same spirit equates "sold out for Jesus" with a certain personality type and a full-time program for fixing the world. We must remember that while we are ambassadors for Christ, we are not his avatars.

Happy Christians in an Anxious Age

It's one of the great paradoxes of our time: almost everything is getting better, but we keep feeling worse. Obviously, there is no shortage of bad news in the world, and on a personal level, things may be especially challenging in your life at the moment. But on a global and historical scale, we live in a remarkable age. It can be hard to tell—both because we get used to the ways things are and because the news mainly talks about bad news—but by almost every conceivable earthly measure, you and I are living in the healthiest, safest, and most prosperous time in the history of the world.

World gross product tripled from 430 billion dollars to 1.2 trillion from 1500 to 1820; then it grew to 3.4 trillion by 1900. In 2018 the global economic output stood at 121 trillion, and it is estimated to be 600 trillion by the end of the century. Global GDP per capita barely increased from the time of Christ until 1800. But following the Industrial Revolution and the introduction of free-market capitalism, GDP per capita began to skyrocket so that the real standard of living across the globe has increased tenfold, and in rich countries much more than that. If you looked at a graph of economic output in the world, the horizontal line would be almost completely flat for most of history; the line would start trending up around 1800 and finally shoot straight up around 1900.

The global population in extreme poverty was at 84 percent in 1830. Today it is at 8.6 percent. Since 1952, global inequality among people and between countries has been decreasing. The percentage of people living in urban slums has decreased sharply on every continent since 1990. People are far wealthier, despite working fewer hours. In 1950 we worked an average of 2,123 hours a year; in 2017 the number was 1,723.

The area covered by trees has been increasing in Asia, Europe, and North America for decades. There are more trees in Europe now than in the Middle Ages.

Since 1960 the number of democracies has been steadily increasing and the number of autocracies has plummeted. There are far fewer wars on the planet than seventy years ago.

The chance of a person dying in a natural catastrophe—earthquake, flood, wildfire, epidemic—has declined 99 percent over the last one hundred years. The global literacy rate in 1820 was 10 percent. Today it is 90 percent. In 1820 average global life expectancy was thirty. Now it is seventy-two. Infant mortality across the globe has plummeted since 1950. The rates of tuberculosis and malaria have fallen sharply since 2000. The number of deaths per one hundred thousand from cancer has been in decline since 1995.

Work-related deaths are down. Child labor is down. In 1800, 60 percent of the nations on the earth had legal slavery. Slavery has been a constant throughout human history, except in the last two hundred years when legalized slavery has become almost nonexistent.

In many ways, the planet is healthier too. CO_2 emissions per dollar of GDP have been falling since 1960. The world produces more oil and has more oil in reserves than in 1980. We use water more efficiently. Access to clean water has increased since 1990 from 75 percent of the world's population to 90 percent. We produce crops in levels unheard of just fifty years ago. Air pollution is declining. Infectious diseases have been decreasing.

In 1900, US households spent 80 percent of expenditures on necessities (food, clothing, housing). Now we spend less than 50 percent, and that is with much bigger homes. The average new home in America in 1900 was 700 square feet; in 1972 it was 1700 square feet; in 2018 it was 2,641 square feet (and this is with much smaller families). Technologies that no one had in 1900 are now in virtually every household in this country and in many countries around the world: electricity, refrigerator, car, indoor plumbing, radio, air-conditioning, washer/dryer, dishwasher, microwave, television, cell phone, digital camera, computer, Internet. In 1800 it took 5.4 hours of work for 1,000 lumen-hours of light. In 1900 it took .22 hours of work. Now it takes .00012 hours of human labor for 1,000 lumen-hours of light. Humans used to have to work hard just to literally keep the lights on; now round-the-clock lighting is a negligible afterthought. Across the globe, we are richer, healthier, and more comfortable, and we live longer than ever before.[11]

But are we happier?

Maybe, maybe not. I sure don't want to go back to working more than half a day a week just to keep the candles going. And yet there is no doubt that anxiety is on the rise. Our wealth has not made us wiser. Our prosperity has not brought us peace of mind. Life is more comfortable, but also more complicated. In theory, we like having nearly limitless options; in reality, we are tied up in knots about what to do, where to live, and whom to marry. We want to be connected to friends and strangers, but then again, maybe we weren't made for around-the-clock comparison and competition. We think we want to have nonstop access to news, information, and opinion, but we also worry what it is doing to our brains, let alone to our souls.

But we have Jesus, right? He can set us free from the fear of death and the worries of life. He can teach us how to live and what to do. He can remind us who we really are. Jesus

---

11 The flurry of figures above is taken from Ronald Bailey and Marian L. Tupy, *Ten Global Trends Every Smart Person Should Know: And Many Others You Will Find Interesting* (Washington, DC: Cato Institute, 2020).

can save us from our sins and show us what really matters in life. If we walk with Jesus, solid joys and lasting treasure are possible.

They most certainly are, but not if we make this whole Christianity thing impossible. Not if we make following Jesus as complicated as filling out your taxes. Not if we make pleasing our heavenly Father as tedious and misanthropic as pleasing Mother Earth. Not if we resign ourselves to spiritual failure instead of licking our lips for a spiritual feast. Life is not easy. Being a Christian is not easy. It is through many tribulations that we must enter the kingdom of God (Acts 14:22). But let us not think that pleasing God is the tribulation, or that Christ means to lay an iron yoke upon our necks, or that the Spirit is only and always grieved by us. Remember, Jesus endured the cross for the *joy* that was set before him (Heb. 12:2).

Benediction

One of the things I love most about being a pastor is also one of the simplest and the shortest. I love pronouncing the benediction at the end of each service. It's far from being a throwaway line meant to dismiss the people to coffee or Sunday school. The benediction is a precious statement of God's blessing upon his people.

The LORD bless you and keep you;
the LORD make his face to shine upon you and be
     gracious to you;
the LORD lift up his countenance upon you and give you
     peace. (Num. 6:24–26)

Those lines are what I say at most services. I stand with my arms spread wide, hoping to be a conduit of God's grace. The people stand, many with their arms outstretched, hoping to capture all that God means to give them. At the close of every service, God's people should be like Jacob: "I will not let you go unless you bless me" (Gen. 32:26).

We all need a benediction, whether we realize it or not. We need to know God is with us. We need to know he sees. We need to know he saves. And we need to know that he smiles upon us.

General Index

Scripture Index

Clearly Reformed

Theology for the Everyday

Learn and grow with thousands of resources
from the ministry of Kevin DeYoung.

Browse articles, sermons, books, podcasts,
and more at **clearlyreformed.org**.

Also Available from Kevin DeYoung

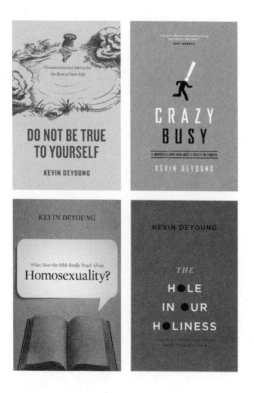